Reconsidering
Jesus of Nazareth

Looking beyond rejection and harmful experiences

David G. R. Keller

D1371923

Ty Noddfa Press

Printed in the United States of America
First Printing, 2020

ISBN 978-0-578-66665-5

Ty Noddfa Press
An imprint of Oasis of Wisdom.net
www.oasisofwisdom.net

For Lauren and Aaron,
whose honest self-knowledge,
moral integrity,
and courage to reconsider Jesus,
inspired my writing.

> "…hearing all that Jesus was doing,
> they came to him in great numbers."
>
> *Mark 3:8*

That was then…

Why would anyone be attracted to Jesus now?

If you believe that compassionate involvement in the lives of other people is needed in our world, then getting to know Jesus may be a worthwhile experience. He invites all of us to have hospitable souls. A hospitable soul is like a home that is always open to the presence of God and our neighbor. Jesus' intimacy with God was the source of his compassionate involvement in the lives of people around him. He ate meals with dishonest tax collectors and sinners and gave healing touch to the sick and blind. He reassured persons in his society who had been shamed and marginalized that they had integrity because they were loved by God. Being a lover of souls was Jesus' highest priority. For him, it was beyond words. The way Jesus *lived* was his message. That's what attracted people to him. But do not take my word for it. Look at his life for yourself. That is the purpose of this little book.

Contents

Foreword

Information and misinformation about Jesus abound. Why yet another book on Jesus? As a former agnostic, now a committed Christian and teacher of biblical studies, and someone who was inflicted with a great deal of misinformation about Jesus for most of my young life, I wish I would have found someone as trustworthy as David Keller much sooner.

David brings the prayerful experiences of a lifetime as Episcopal priest, retreat director, teacher, researcher and shepherd of a contemplative community to this book. It is truly a work of hard labor as well as a work of love. Too many books about Jesus are either restricted to historical research alone or to a portrait of the author's devotion to Jesus. David integrates those two paths in a way that expresses humbly to the reader the best we can know about who Jesus was and is.

As a biblical scholar I know that historical reconstructions of the historical Jesus rest on a number of complex probable judgments. David's use of the historical scholarship on Jesus and his context avoids speculative hypotheses while benefitting from aspects that have wide consensus. This book performs a difficult task while making it look easy: it distills and incorporates the best scholarly thinking about Jesus within a prayerful and faith-filled exploration of Jesus. And this is as it should be, for we know Jesus only through the testimony of those who found forgiveness and new life in him and in the mystery of his death and resurrection that is the culmination of his human journey. Any attempt, therefore, to introduce readers to the deeper meaning and significance of Jesus' life and message should be attentive to the first century Jewish and Roman context as well as the longing for God that finds in him the consoling and challenging love of God, as David's work is.

David's voice is direct, clear, and prayerful, inviting the reader into a pilgrimage in which the mind can be illuminated by a passionate heart yearning for God. He is a spiritual guide to return to again and again.

Pamela Hedrick, Ph.D.
Author of *Do You Now Believe.* Wipf&Stock, 2017

Preface

"Now among those who went up to worship at the
[Passover] *festival were some Greeks.*
They came to Philip, who was from Bethsaida in Galilee,
and said to him, 'Sir, we wish to see Jesus.'" (John 12:20–21)

Most people have heard about Jesus of Nazareth, but many are surprised to learn that he was a devout first-century Jew, not a "Christian." *Reconsidering Jesus of Nazareth* is written for persons who do not know much about him and for others who for various reasons have lost interest in Jesus. I hope to give readers an overview of some essential aspects of Jesus' life in the context of his own society and Jewish faith community.

If you are already familiar with traditional teaching about Jesus and the significance of his life, parts of this little book will seem repetitious. Although it may affirm and add some detail to what you already know, keep in mind that the format and content of *Reconsidering Jesus of Nazareth* is intended for persons who are curious about Jesus yet know very little about him and may not know where to look for a concise portrait of his life.

It will not be possible in this limited space to go into a lot of detail, but I hope this portrait of Jesus will encourage readers to explore more of his life. My choice of topics in each chapter has been based on recurring questions and concerns expressed by a variety of persons throughout my ministry as teacher and priest. Since these interests are interrelated and some readers may be less familiar with Christian theology and the Bible, I have chosen to repeat portions of some fundamental content throughout the book. I hope this repetition is helpful.

I am a lifelong follower of Jesus Christ and have been an Episcopal priest for fifty-seven years. Some Christians have questioned the authenticity of my life with God, declaring that I am not a Christian because I will not accept their theological formulas about Jesus and "salvation." I am not alone. I know persons who have been turned away from Jesus because portions of the Old and New Testaments of the Bible have been used by Christians to judge them and cast shame on their way of life. Too many persons have been alienated, emotionally abused, or angered by judgmental pronouncements in the name of God. Others are repelled by conflicts between Christians, religious wars waged in the name of Christ, and prejudice based on teaching presented as Christian. Love has been preempted by coercion. Freedom has been replaced by fear, confusion, or restriction. Far too often Jesus, himself, has been hidden underneath layers of words about Jesus that sometimes misrepresent his life and teaching. But Jesus is more than words about Jesus.

I am convinced that frequently the Christian path has been abandoned because it has been presented in ways that distort its positive and transformative way of life.

Some of the skepticism about Jesus or dismissal of his relevance takes place without opportunities to get to know him as a devout first-century Jew and to observe his compassionate and inclusive engagement with the needs of people around him. It is my hope that *Reconsidering Jesus of Nazareth* will provide an opportunity to encounter Jesus in this wider context.

Reconsidering Jesus of Nazareth may also be helpful in Christian faith communities to introduce inquirers to the life of Jesus, as well as a resource for spiritual formation of youth and adults. They, too, will benefit from discovering Jesus in the context of his culture and religious life.

David Keller
Feast of the Epiphany 2020

Introduction

Our original nature

I want to begin by sharing some of my responses to real-life situations where literal interpretations of the Bible have been used by Christians in ways that have caused personal anxiety, pain, and doubt in other persons. In some cases, the response has been rejection of Jesus and Christianity. I hope these narratives and my responses will inspire conversations and reconsideration about Jesus' understanding of human life, what God is like, how God responds to human sin, and whether or not the Christian path is the only true religion. Later chapters present other issues, based on conversations I have had with persons, mostly young adults. Some were raised in Christian families with conservative beliefs. They can no longer accept what they were taught and are asking serious questions and looking for guidance. My approach is not "liberal" vs. "conservative." It is to seek, in community, an authentic understanding of biblical texts in their original contexts that will guide our lives today.

In the remainder of *Reconsidering Jesus of Nazareth*, Chapter 1 describes Jesus' Jewish life of prayer and ministry as the source and vocation of Christian living. Chapters 2 and 3 describe Jesus' early life and ministry as narrated in the gospels of Matthew, Mark, Luke, and John. Chapters 4 and 5 describe Jesus' understanding of power and his passion for life. Chapters 6 and 7 include the author's responses to some primary questions and concerns people have expressed about Jesus' death and the Christian understanding of God's threefold nature as Trinity. Chapters 8 and 9 discuss ways Jesus is present in the lives of modern Christians and options for persons who want to explore the possibility of following Jesus today. I invite readers to look at the table of contents and begin where you are most interested. Chapters 3 and 4 will be helpful for readers who know little about the life of Jesus. I encourage you to make notes about your own experience as you read and keep track of questions that arise.

A very simple message

Jesus' life and ministry is based on a positive outlook on human life. He entrusted his followers with a very simple message. *The original nature of human life is goodness that flows from and is sustained by intimacy with God.* This radical claim declares that God was uniquely present in Jesus and that his life proclaims the sanctity and ultimate purpose of human life. Jesus knew from his Jewish heritage that the source of this original nature is God's love and creative energy. He proclaimed that our human vocation is to participate in the life of God and make that unity tangible in the way we live. Jesus' life demonstrates that authentic human nature unfolds in the context of creation, among people, within time and space, yet is eternal because God is eternal.

The unfolding of our original nature is never forced on us. On the contrary, we can both ignore or reject the gifts of goodness and intimacy with God. We cannot envision or attain the fullness of our being on our own or all at once. Therefore, we search for God with restless hearts. God's love remains unconditional during this journey. It is not always easy, and sometimes we take a wrong turn or are given poor directions. But we are always loved.

This is good news to many people, but not all Christians will agree with its message.

How do we know what God is like?

In the early 1970s I was living in an Athabaskan Indian village on the Yukon River in Alaska. One day I was out in the mountains west of the Yukon hunting caribou with a friend. This was not for sport. It was to help feed our families during the cold winter. We were on a ridge high in the mountains waiting for a herd of caribou to pass close to us when my friend turned and said out of the blue, "You are a priest and all that. But I don't believe any of it. It all goes back to when I was a child." When I asked, "What happened?" he replied, "It was Willtist! That mean old man up in the sky with a big fist that willtist I do this and willtist I don't do that, or else. I didn't want anything to do with a god like that!" When we returned to the village and had supper in his log cabin, he drew me a sketch of Willtist, a scary old bearded male face with a strong arm and big fist looking down on us from a puffy cloud. That intimidating image was still with him as an adult. I still have his sketch. I have met too many people with a similar understanding of God instilled by adults in their vulnerable minds as children.

But is that what God is really like? Are human beings bad from the beginning? Do we have to become "good" or face the consequences? Many people today live in an environment of psychological or religious fear. They have been told that God is angry and will punish anyone who does not change their way of living or affirm a specific statement of faith in Jesus and become a Christian.

The Bible presents a different point of view. The Hebrew Scriptures (the Old Testament) begin with the proclamation that goodness is the original nature of human life. At the end of a narrative in the book of Genesis in which God creates major aspects of the world as we know it, including human beings, these words repeat a constant theme: "God saw everything he had made, and indeed, it was very good."[1] In an earlier verse the same narrative states: "So God created humankind in his image, in the image of God he created them; male and female he created them."[2] The image of God is also part of the original nature of every person. It is an indelible sign of the ultimate meaning and purpose of human life.

Where does sin enter the journey?

At this point some readers may ask "But what about sin?" Yes, sin is a reality in all our lives and is not what God desires for human life. In a first century letter to other Christians, one of the earliest followers of Jesus wrote "If we say that we have no sin, we deceive ourselves, and the truth is not in us."[3] The way you and I live does matter. What is sinful behavior? The Bible is very clear that "sin" is willfully denying what God desires for human life. It is unrestrained control of our own lives, especially if we cause harm or worse to other people. This self-centered approach to life causes harm to ourselves and alienates us from other people and from God.

What is repentance?

Sinful behavior does not change the fact that God's love for us is unconditional. This is a theme that reappears throughout the Bible. God reacts negatively to sin not to condemn, but to seek reconciliation. God's desire is proclaimed in graphic language in a dialogue with the Hebrew prophet Ezekiel: "Have I any pleasure in the death of the wicked, says the Lord God, and not rather that they should turn from their ways and live?"[4] Ezekiel describes repentance as turning *away from* our control of life *toward* God's desire for reconciliation. Repentance is turning toward God and God's desires for human life. Yes, repentance may reflect our remorse for sinful behavior, but it does not require "beating ourselves up." Repentance is a genuine longing to return to our original goodness and relationship with God. Repentance is positive!

After describing the grievous hurt Israel's sins have caused, the prophet Jeremiah speaks in poetic language of God's unconditional love and desire to forgive the people's sins, "I have loved you with an everlasting love; therefore I have continued my faithfulness to you." [5] The Old Testament psalms are filled with references to the consequences of sin as well as the constant desire of

God to forgive and guide repentant sinners on a path to renewed life. In the New Testament gospel of John, Jesus is present when religious leaders catch a woman committing adultery and want to punish her to death by stoning. After Jesus confronts them with the reality of their own sins they turn away. Then he turns to the woman and says, "Nor do I condemn you. Go your way, and from now on do not sin again."[6] The woman is offered forgiveness and encouragement rather than condemnation. I hope these few examples demonstrate the constant theme in the Bible of the reality of human sin and God's constant forgiveness prompted by unconditional love.

My Alaskan friend thought that "Willtist" was a coercive and vengeful god. The biblical witness proclaims a compassionate God. The message is clear: there is nothing you or I can do to make God love us more than God loves us right now. And there is nothing we can do to make God love us less than God loves us at this moment. This means that our lives do not have to "measure up" to warrant God's love or that we have to accept, without reservation, a specific Christian doctrinal statement to "go to heaven."

What are you thinking right now? What would you say to my Alaskan friend?

Is God's unconditional love for everyone?

I have a friend whose nephew is a devout Jew. He is happily married to a woman who loves him dearly. They have two small children. She is a Christian who has been taught and believes firmly that persons who are not Christians must "accept" Jesus Christ in order to go heaven. Her dilemma is real; yet her husband sees no reason to abandon his Jewish religious life that has its roots in the heritage of Jesus of Nazareth, a first century Jew. The wife's dilemma is shared by many Christians and raises a fundamental issue among world religious traditions. Is there only "one way" or do many paths and differing experiences lead to the same truth?

I wrestled with this question for a long time. I grew up in a devout Christian family and did not encounter other religious traditions until I was a young adult. I was committed to Jesus of Nazareth and the uniqueness of Christian experience. I lacked both knowledge and experience of other traditions until I was introduced to them in college and seminary and through some of my friends. I began to ask myself "What is unique about Christian experience?" and "Does uniqueness infer exclusivity?" It has been difficult for me to respond to these questions. Like many people I enjoyed my study of other religious traditions. But I was looking at them through the lenses of my Christian belief and experience. I considered myself "accepting" of other religious belief and piety. I realize now that my attitude was quite patronizing.

Learning the difference between uniqueness and exclusivity

A moment of truth convinced me that uniqueness does not infer exclusivity. It came in in the mid-1970s during my doctoral study in the School of Education at New York University in Washington Square, Manhattan. My focus was religious education and I found myself studying with and getting to know students from Judaism, Islam, Hinduism, Moonies, Buddhism, Shinto, and the New Age. It was a kaleidoscope's view of humankind's experience of God. My best friend during this two-year period was a Buddhist priest from Korea. Once we stayed up all night in his apartment celebrating the Buddha's birthday with traditional Korean food. Later he visited my family on Long Island and we had many late-night discussions. I was criticized by some Christian friends for welcoming him in my home and "exposing" my children to his influence.

Part of my studies at NYU was with a disciple of Swami Vivekananda, a Hindu guru in Manhattan. His teaching was filled with wisdom and his boundaries for seeking truth were transparent, even though some of it seemed foreign to me. Later in the NYU library, as I summarized what I was learning from him, I went into a state of panic. "What if he is right?" Suddenly my Christian belief and experience seemed challenged. How could Christianity and Hinduism both be "right?" I was afraid I would have to choose between the two traditions in order to accept "what is true." After several weeks of discernment, the Christian New Testament came to my rescue. Saint Paul, in his letters to some of the earliest Christian communities reminded me that God has been revealing God's self since the beginning of human life. God is not limited in the ways God may be known. Saint Paul helped me realize the distinction between *uniqueness* and *exclusivity*. He was very firm in his statements about the uniqueness of the identity of Jesus Christ and the uniqueness of what he makes possible for human life. But he realized that Christian experience does not exhaust the manifestations of the wisdom and power of God. I was not only relieved. I was liberated! I was relieved and liberated because I could accept the integrity of my own Christian path and the integrity of the Swami's path as well. We did not agree on everything, but I learned that neither tradition may claim sole access to the Truth or claim to be the only venue for God's presence in the universe. I am unapologetically Christian to the roots of my being. At the same time my Christian path has been and continues to be enlightened and strengthened by God's presence in the wisdom and practice of other traditions. It is not the only venue for life with God.

What is your experience with the distinction between uniqueness and exclusivity?

Is God present in some places but not in others?

From 1961 until 1968 I was a priest and pastor in Shageluk, Alaska among the Ingalik tribe of Athabaskan Indians. Almost every person in the village was a Christian and the Episcopal Church had been present in this area for over 100 years. In the middle of a sub-zero night in December 1962 there was a frantic pounding on the door of my log cabin. I had just gone to sleep after participating in part of an annual mask dance in the village kashime, a semi-underground gathering place. The mask dance is an annual winter solstice celebration of the creation of the animals, birds, fish, and berries that sustain the lives of the Ingalik people. It also offers songs of prayer to the spirits of these creatures for their returned sustenance in the coming year. The kashime is decorated to depict the natural world that nourishes the lives of the people. It is some of the finest liturgy I have ever experienced with masked dancers representing each type of creature and loud singing and drumming. It was an exciting celebration of life during a very cold and dark time of year. I left the all-night celebration at about 2 AM to get some sleep.

When I opened the door to my cabin, Grandpa Joe, came in. He was as agitated as any human being I have ever seen. Joe was the kashime leader and a good friend. When I asked, "Joe, what's wrong?" he shouted, "That man up there (pointing to the home of the conservative evangelical pastor in the village) came and said, 'God is not in the kashime!'" Then Joe, asked, "Is he right?" I said, "I'm not the one to decide. Only you and the people can decide." Joe replied with great emotion, "If we do not do what we do in the kashime we are all the same as dogs, we just eat, sleep, work and shit!" His response was one of the most poignant theological statements I have ever heard. In his mind, as a devoted Christian, the indigenous religious life of the village still had deep meaning, purpose and a divine connection.

Was God present in the kashime or not? What do you think? I knew that only Joe and other Christians in the village could decide whether or not parts of their centuries-old religious life were compatible with following Jesus.

Context is essential for understanding the Bible

Some readers will assert that God is not present in other religious traditions. For example, I have been in discussions with Christians who believe firmly that Christianity is the only way based on the following verses in the tenth and fourteenth chapters of the gospel of John.

In John's tenth chapter, when religious leaders question Jesus' claim that the source of his words and actions come from God, Jesus replies *"The Father and I are one."* (John 10:31) Some Christians say this "proves" that Jesus is God and that Christianity

is the only way to God. I am convinced that such a literal interpretation misses the point Jesus was making. Jesus realized that
his experience of intimacy with God was the source of all his wisdom and actions. When he said, *"The Father and I are one."* he was
referring to his intimacy with God and the truth about authentic
human life. Jesus wanted all persons to experience this same intimacy. He prayed to the Holy One: *"…that they be one as you and I
are one."* (John 17:11) He knew that his experience of life was what
God desired for all human beings. Later, he would say to God,
*"The glory that you have given me I have given them, so that they
may be one, as we are one, I in them and you in me, that they may be
completely one…"* (John 17:22) Jesus did not demand that people
agree with his teaching. He gave them the opportunity to follow
him into fullness of human life: intimacy and union with God. It
was Jesus' experience of God's love that enabled him to love others.

In John's fourteenth chapter, *"Jesus said to [Thomas], 'I am the
way, and the truth, and the life. No one comes to the Father except
through me. If you know me, you will know my Father, also. From
now on you do know him and have seen him."* (John 14:6-7)

Later in the chapter, *"Philip said to [Jesus], 'Lord, show us the
Father, and we will be satisfied.' Jesus said to him, 'Have I been with
you all this time, Philip, and you still do not know me? Whoever has
seen me has seen the Father. How can you say, "Show us the Father?'
Do you not believe that I am in the Father and the Father is in me?
The words that I say to you I do not speak on my own; but the Father
who dwells in me does his works."'* (John 14:8-10)

If these words are taken literally, and out of context, they may
be used to justify Christianity as the only way to a relationship with
God. But Jesus did not speak these words for that purpose. *He was
speaking to his Jewish disciples, not to 21st century Christians.* Jesus
knew that some religious authorities feared his popularity and his
interpretations of the Torah. They worried that if Jesus' popularity
created unrest in Jerusalem their Roman occupiers would forbid
the practice of their religion. They had been plotting to kill Jesus
for more than a year. Jesus knew that his mission to restore fidelity

to the covenant Israel had made with God and his compassionate and inclusive engagement with the needs of people around him, especially the poor, the ill, and sinners could lead to his death. He was willing to take that risk to be faithful to the words and desires he had heard from his Father.

As the great feast of the Jewish Passover came closer, Jesus gathered his closest disciples to prepare them for his death. He spoke of going away to a place they would eventually come, yet they were confused. Thomas asked Jesus to show them the way. Jesus knew he would return to his Father (God) and that his anxious disciples would eventually follow. *"I am the way..."* is Jesus reassurance that when Jesus dies and returns to his Father, that same path is open to the disciples who do not understand what Jesus is saying. It is clear to me after decades of meditation on the four gospels and consultation with a variety of Jewish and Christian biblical scholars that Jesus' words in these verses were spoken to persons who had placed their lives in Jesus' hands. In the wake of his possible death they were confused and seriously anxious about his and their future. After Jesus' death and resurrection two of the disciples were headed back home dejected and embarrassed. They had left family and livelihood to follow Jesus and now their future was uncertain. As they walked a man appeared and asked why they looked so depressed. Not recognizing Jesus, one of them said to him *"But we had hoped that he was the one to redeem Israel."* (Luke 24:21) This response gives us some idea of the extreme anxiety and disappointment Jesus' followers experienced before and after his death.

The path, and Jesus' determination to be faithful to what he has learned from God, leads to what is true and life-giving. What Jesus has heard from his Father is the *truth*. It is the source of authentic and abundant human life. *"I came that they may have life, and have it abundantly."* (John 10:10)

Jesus assures those who have left so much to follow him that this "way" he has learned from his intimacy with God *will lead them, also, to that same intimacy.* Intimacy with God is the "way" that leads to the truth and is the source of abundant human life. In other words, "If you want to become one with God, place your lives in my hands and become like me." Jesus' quiet times of prayer were the source of his intimacy with God. Jesus wanted the same flow of God's life that was in him to flow in every person.

As we have seen, the encounters with God that Jesus experienced in his constant prayer became the source of his words and actions. This means that Jesus' life and teaching made God's life tangible. *"If you know me, you will know my Father, also. From now on you do know him and have seen him."* is not a theological statement! Jesus is speaking about his experience of God and what it demonstrates about God's nature.

Philip is still puzzled by Jesus' words. He rephrases Thomas' question and asks *"Lord, show us the Father, and we will be satisfied."* Jesus is patient yet reminds Philip that throughout his ministry there were many opportunities for Philip and others to see God's presence in Jesus' words and actions. *"Have I been with you all this time, Philip, and you still do not know me? Whoever has seen me has seen the Father. How can you say, 'Show us the Father?'"* Once again, Jesus is not "talking theology." He is saying that the presence of God is palpable and dwells within his life and his compassionate engagement in the lives of persons in his society.

A very simple message

It is worth repeating. Goodness is our original nature and God is the source of this goodness. Jesus' life announces that human beings are created to be in eternal communion with the fullness of God. That is our original nature and Jesus' daily life demonstrates what communion with God looks like. His great desire was, and is, that every person shares this same union with God. Sinful behavior does alienate a person from this communion, but never negates the original goodness of each human life. How do we know this?

An Invitation to see and hear all that Jesus was doing

A first step is to explore who Jesus was in the context of his first-century Jewish culture and why his words and actions motivated people to come to him in great numbers. Only then will we be able to discover whether Jesus is worth reconsidering today.

Jesus' primary way of teaching was the way he lived. He had an open and hospitable soul. His life was his message. What was that life like? The four New Testament gospels will help you see for yourself. The next three chapters will guide you through a brief summary of these gospels and give you an opportunity to look deeper into Jesus' life of prayer, his active life, and his teaching. What influence can this first-century Jew have on us in the twenty-first century? His life will speak for itself.

Chapter 1

Jesus' Jewish Life of Prayer and Ministry: The Source and Vocation of Christian Living

Embracing the unknown

Thirty years ago I was having a conversation with a well-known astrophysicist who was near retirement. I asked him "What is the most significant thing you have learned in all these years of studying the universe?" Without hesitation he replied, "What we see, even with the best telescopes, is so little of what is there."

Recent research has determined that "what we see" and experience is only five percent of what exists. The rest is mystery that cosmologists have named "dark matter" and "dark energy." This means that our Milky Way galaxy and its billions of stars, millions more galaxies and our solar system are next to nothing in our vast universe. Our massive sun, ninety-three million miles from earth, is only an "average" size star and our planet home is tiny compared to our solar system neighbors Saturn and Jupiter. Several years ago, as it was orbiting Saturn, NASA's Cassini space craft took a photograph of the earth. We are a tiny blue and white orb floating in a vast black sea of space, reflecting the light of our sun.

This is the physical context for life on earth. It is one way of seeing and describing what we call reality. We are indescribably small and surrounded and influenced by matter and energy we do not yet fully understand.

What are you thinking right now? Is physical reality all there is? Where does human life fit into this vast context?

Is there a wider context for human life?

Is the earth, eclipsed by the vastness of the 13.8 billion-year-old universe, only an accidental leftover from the interstellar matter that formed our sun? Does human life as we experience it end when we die? And are human beings and other life forms on earth simply products of a long-term natural process that evolved into life on our planet today? What are your thoughts?

Many people would say "yes." They do not deny the beauty and wonder of the earth and the pleasures, complexity, challenges and tragedies of human life. At the same time they are convinced that life as we know it is all there is. When we die it is over. This is a reasonable point of view. It does not necessarily deny the goodness of human life and the need for responsible and moral values. Yet, almost always, this perspective leaves out the possibility for anything else but human initiative and creativity. Although there is room for mystery in life there is rarely acknowledgement of a spiritual dimension. How do you respond to this point of view? Where in this physical context can you and I find meaning and purpose for our lives?

A spiritual context for human life

Among the world's religious traditions the Jewish heritage provides a unique spiritual context for human life that complements and completes this vast physical context. It is another and complementary way that sees reality as the sacred creation of a divine being. The good news is that it is a very "down to earth" vision that became tangible in the life of a devout first-century Jew, Jesus of Nazareth. Jesus' Jewish heritage was firmly based in experience of God rather than theological reflection. The context for Jesus' life combined the richness of his Jewish heritage with the daily lives of people he encountered.

A threshold to the spiritual dimension of reality

Although there are external influences, the journey into the spiritual dimension is always personal. When I was fourteen I remember going outside on a pitch black night when the Milky Way almost filled the sky and seemed close enough to gather a handful of stars. Romantic, yes, but I already knew a lot about physics and had built my first Newtonian telescope when I was thirteen. In retrospect I realize now that I was being led beyond my emotion and knowledge. What I was experiencing lured me beyond my usual desire to define and control what was happening as well as the outcome. I still remember, at eighty-two, the experience of awe that without any decision on my part led to immense gratitude. I already believed in God, but this experience transcended cognitive affirmation. The focus was not on me. My sense of wonder was a mutual experience. Letting go of my control to discern what was happening opened me to God's initiative. I was freed to hear God's Spirit speak without my conscious thought determining what the message should be. Over the years this mysterious form of listening has given unexpected meaning to my worship, study, and prayer.

Since that adolescent experience I have learned from incidents in Jesus' life and his parables that he, too, was led as a child and adult, into the spiritual dimension. He used mundane images from daily life to speak of God's presence in life: kneading bread, sowing seed, wild flowers, mustard seed, and water. Various other narratives in the Christian New Testament gospels of Matthew, Mark, Luke, and John describe how Jesus was fundamentally rooted in his Jewish heritage through continued reflection on the Hebrew scriptures and participation in the variety of religious celebrations that gave life to his Jewish religious tradition. The tap root that energized this heritage and made it tangible in Jesus' daily life and relationships was his personal prayer. In a constant pattern of quiet listening he experienced the presence of God. It was an intimate experience that integrated his humanity with the mystery of God's nature and gave meaning, purpose and energy to his life.

Both Jewish and Christian traditions have learned that through a discipline of quiet listening a person may become aware of the spiritual dimension of life. Jews and Christians agree that the spiritual dimension is the movement of God's energy, often called the Holy Spirit, giving and sustaining life throughout creation. The spiritual dimension is always present but we are not always receptive. Prayer becomes openness to God's presence and a willingness to respond.

In the early Christian tradition, a Syrian desert monk named Pseudo-Macarius described prayer in this way: "As near as the body is to the soul…so much nearer is God present, to come and open the locked door of the heart and to fill us with heavenly riches."[7] One of the most revered modern Jewish teachers was Abraham Joshua Heschel. He wrote: "Prayer takes the mind out of the narrowness of self-interest, and enables us to see the world in the mirror of the holy…To pray is to regain a sense of the mystery that animates all beings, the divine margin in all attainments."[8]

The flow of energy in prayer, in its varieties of personal and corporate expressions and venues, is a threshold to the spiritual dimension of life.

The evolution of the Christian tradition

Jesus offered the same intimacy and power of God that he experienced within the rich well of the Jewish spiritual tradition to all persons who were willing to entrust their lives to God's presence in him. The first women and men who responded were fellow Jews. In Jesus' words and actions they could recognize God's presence in a palpable way. All kinds of people found the energizing flow of God's Spirit in their encounters with Jesus. Their lives were not the same and this gave birth to a strong desire to remember their encounters with Jesus and share with other people the fullness of life they experienced with him. After Jesus' death and resurrection they became known as "Followers of the Way" and eventually included many persons who were not Jewish. The memories of Jesus' life and ministry in a variety of small faith communities were used for teaching and worship that eventually were included in the four New Testament gospels.

During his lifetime, Jesus had no intention of replacing Judaism with a new religious tradition.

As communities of followers of Jesus gradually included persons who were not Jews it was necessary to interpret the causes and meaning of his death and resurrection using images and language from the dominant Greek culture of the Mediterranean world. Some Jewish leaders insisted that all followers of Jesus become Jews and follow Jewish religious customs, other leaders did not. These necessary issues of corporate life led to confrontations, theological disagreements, misunderstandings, and conflict that eventually resulted in a split into two religious traditions. Eventually, Followers of the Way, who now included persons who were not Jewish, became known as "Christians."

Although the initial disagreements that led to the split were between Jews and Jewish Followers of the Way, eventually some Christian leaders and teachers who were not Jews criticized and judged Jews who rejected Jesus as the long awaited Messiah. In some cases Jews who did not follow Jesus were blamed (inaccurately) for the death of Jesus. Sadly, these nascent anti-Jewish perspectives in the early centuries of the Christian tradition have persisted and been used to justify modern anti-Semitism. Although these negative perspectives about Jews are contrary to the life and teaching of Jesus, and in far too many cases have resulted in horrible atrocities, they do not represent the relationships of all Christians with Jews.

Further discussion of the long and complex history that led to the evolution of two separate traditions is beyond the scope of this book.[9]

Jewish roots are the foundation of the Christian tradition

The circumstances that led to the formation of a separate Christian tradition should not cloud the fact that Christian life has deep and essential roots in Jewish scriptures, worship, prayer, and Jewish experiences of the relationship between human beings and God. One of the most fundamental roots is the spiritual formation of

Jesus as a first century Jew. His Jewishness is an authentic guide for the formation and life of Christians.

The vocation of people who follow Jesus within the Christian tradition is to transmit, share and mentor the same relationship Jesus had with God, whom he called "the living Father." (John 6:57) Jesus entire life and identity was formed by and flowed from his intimacy with his living Father (John 14:8-10). Jesus' awareness of God's presence filled every moment and situation of his daily life. Intimacy with God was the source of his desires, teaching, and compassionate engagement in the lives of other people. It was the wellspring of the authority, energy, and wisdom that attracted and transformed their lives.

The vocation of Christianity

The purpose of the Christian tradition, its denominations and local congregations is not the preservation of its institutional life and programs as ends in themselves. The vocation of each Christian church in every new generation is to transmit the experience of God present in Jesus of Nazareth to its members so that their lives make Jesus Christ tangible in the way they live. The tangible presence of Jesus in the lives of individual Christians may be called **Christness**.[10] Jesus invites us to participate in the nature and life of God present in his life. It is not a personal achievement. Christness is an opportunity to collaborate with God's spirit to gradually become a manifestation of God's presence and grace in a sacred, yet troubled world. The core of Christianity is Christness not the institution. The institution is called together by God's spirit to become an environment that inspires and supports Christness. When a person sees the presence of Jesus in another person's manner of life there is less need for words about Jesus in books like this one. Early in the evolution of the Christian church an Egyptian monk named Pachomius said, "If you see a [person] pure and humble, it is a great vision. For what is greater than such a vision, to see the Invisible God in a visible [person], His temple?"[11]

The vocation and responsibilities of Christness

Christness is always freely chosen. God does not superimpose or coerce God's self on you or me. If we seek this vocation, Christness is an opportunity to let our lives be places where God chooses to dwell. The presence of God in our lives will transform the way we live. It will not happen all at once and its focus is not totally on us. It brings responsibilities and challenges for taking our part in healing and restoring a chaotic and broken world.[12]

But how do we know what Christness is like and how does it become a reality in our lives?

The origin and nature of our Christness

In order to embrace the reality of Christness in each new generation it is essential to see its origin in the life of Jesus. This will give a glimpse of the importance of what follows in the rest of this little book. Jesus was convinced that God's presence was breaking forth into the lives of the people of Israel during his lifetime to restore their commitment to God's desires for human life (the Torah.) He called this "the reign of God" (sometimes translated "the kingdom of God") and exhorted people around him to join in this mission. This was his gospel (the good news). It began with the transformation of the lives of persons who had the greatest needs. Jesus walked throughout the towns and villages healing the sick, assuring people of God's love and forgiveness, and speaking out about the challenge to make justice and compassion tangible in society and religious life. Jesus exhorted people to join him in what God was making possible through his life. He was clear that this was God's activity and he exhorted a sacrificial response and commitment from all who would entrust their lives to God's presence in his life.

Jesus makes it clear that the reign of God is not his doing. It is God's initiative. That is his good news, his gospel. We shall see in later chapters that he invites people who are drawn to him to be open to the same indwelling power of God present in his life and challenges them to make the consequences of the reign of God a reality in people's lives. This is the two-fold nature of Christness: to make Christ's life tangible in our daily lives and to share in establishing the reign of God.

Jesus knew that complete commitment to the reign of God would be costly and dangerous. Jesus knew that execution would be an almost certain consequence of his spiritual path and teaching. He did not accept this without difficult interior struggle. Jesus accepted death because he would not deny his true self and mission in order to appease the self-serving power of some of the religious and political leaders of his day. Jesus' love for all those around him, including those who condemned him, was too powerful to allow false values to prevail over his personal experience of true human life. He accepted death to stand firm for authentic life. He was practicing what he preached. His non-violent response to those who chose to execute him was a powerful statement that he knew they had no idea of the emptiness of their values and power. He told them, "My power is not of this world."

Why is Jesus called Jesus Christ?

Some readers already know that "Christ" comes from the Greek word "Kristos," meaning a person who has been anointed. Yet there are many people who are unsure about why Jesus is called Christ. Who anointed him and for what purpose?

The Greek word "Kris" means to smear and is almost always used in reference to a sacred act of anointing with olive oil. "Kristos" or "Christ" in the New Testament is used with the name Jesus to claim that Jesus is "the anointed one." The New Testament gospels and epistles used "Kristos" in place of the Hebrew word "mashiyah" meaning "anointed one." It is the derivation of the English word "messiah." In the Hebrew scriptures kings and prophets were anointed with oil for their sacred functions to care for God's people, Israel. Usually they were chosen and anointed because the spirit of God had already "rested on their shoulders" and gave them power to serve the people on behalf of God. In like manner, when Jesus was baptized in the Jordan River the spirit of God rested on his shoulders and Jesus became "an anointed one." (Matthew 3:13-17 & Mark 9:1-11) Soon after his baptism Jesus became aware that God was breaking into the lives of the people of Israel to restore them to faithful fulfillment of God's desires for human life as revealed in the Torah.

Luke's gospel narrates that soon after Jesus baptism and temptations in the wilderness he began to travel to the villages and towns in Galilee because Jesus interpreted his anointing as being congruent with the vision of the Hebrew prophets that God would unite all Israel's people and free people who were burdened by illness or rejected by society. When Jesus was preaching in his home town of Nazareth on the Sabbath Luke narrates that Jesus proclaimed that he was the fulfillment of these words from the prophet Isaiah:

"The Spirit of the Lord is upon me, because he has anointed me to bring good news to the poor. He has sent me to proclaim release to the captives and recovery of sight to the blind, to let the oppressed go free, to proclaim the year of the Lord's favor." (Luke 4:18-19)

Jesus saw his anointing with the spirit of God as a mission to make God's restoration of Israel tangible through his words and actions. *"But if it is by the finger of God that I cast out demons, then the kingdom of God has come to you."* (Luke 11:20)

The earliest followers of Jesus knew him as "the anointed one" and in the Greek New Testament gospels and epistles he is called "Christ." A person who makes Jesus' life tangible in their life shares in his Christness.

The challenge of Christness

Jesus was passionate to share his experience of God and the vision of fullness of life it revealed with every person who desired to entrust their lives to him. His promise was very simple. By embracing God's presence in his life a person would receive the gift of participating in the nature of God.[13] The divine power and presence that was united with Jesus' humanity will be given to us. St. Paul describes this gift that transformed his life in this way: "I have been crucified with Christ; and it is no longer I who live, but it is Christ who lives in me." (Galatians 2:19b-20a). It is normal to ask, "But, what about me? Do I have to disappear?" The answer is "yes" and "no." Jesus' response is very clear. If we maintain control of our lives we actually lose the life God created us to have. It's a matter of context. We can live according to our definition of a full and meaningful life. We can set the stage for living our life or we can let go of control and gradually entrust ourselves to God's vision for fullness of life.

What does "letting go of control of our lives" really mean? Is it weakness? Are we left out of the process of living? What happens to our initiative? What about our creative talents? Jesus' response is very simple. He exhorted his followers to experience authentic human life by freely making their own wishes congruent with God's desires for human life. He knew from his own experience that self-emptying and openness of heart makes room for the presence of God in a person's life and enables them to communicate that presence to others. Rather than limiting a person's life, it brings joy and freedom that are the offspring of love.

Letting go of control of our lives makes it possible to share in the life of God. We do not lose the uniqueness of who we are any more than St. Paul stopped being who he was when his passion to persecute followers of Jesus was transformed to proclaiming fullness of life in Christ through a personal experience of the risen Jesus. Yet all that we are is transformed by the presence of the same divine life that made Jesus an authentic human being. Christness is fullness of human life because the life of Jesus, the Christ, shows us what human life is meant to be. In other words, What God is like is revealed in Jesus' human life so that our human lives may share in the nature of God.

The mind of Jesus Christ

But how can we recognize and begin the journey to fullness of life? St. Paul exhorted followers of Jesus to have "the mind of Christ." What did he mean? The Greek word for "mind" is "nous." It means the human ability to discern God's presence and what God desires.

I am convinced that Paul's exhortation was a challenge to some of the earliest followers of Jesus to discover the same view of reality and desires that motivated Jesus' words and actions. Paul was inviting people to share Jesus' experience of life because he saw life in the same way that God sees life. This was and remains the consciousness of Jesus.

Consciousness is the window or lens through which a person perceives her or his interior and exterior life. It is the way we "see life." It is experience, not thought. This "frame" of awareness shapes a person's knowledge, relationships, and actions. It will influence the development of a person's core values. Consciousness is an essential aspect of our life with God, other persons, our work, families, society, and creation. This "vision" of life shapes our judgments, decisions, and behavior. Therefore, consciousness is a fundamental and practical part of getting things done and doing them well. The formation of our consciousness will determine how we live, and move, and have our being.

The four canonical gospels present a portrait of the consciousness of Jesus.[14] Jesus taught that authentic knowledge of God flows from experience of and union with God. Once God is known from personal experience, God's presence and wisdom are recognized everywhere in life. This is what Jesus meant when he said, "If you know me, you will know my Father also. From now on you do know him and have seen him." (John 14:7) People who listened to Jesus' teaching experienced his consciousness of God. "Now when Jesus had finished saying these things, the crowds were astounded at his teaching, for he taught them as one having authority, and not as their scribes." (Matthew 7:28-29) But how does our consciousness become congruent with the way God, in Jesus' life, sees and encounters the world?

Is Christness worthwhile? What will it make possible?

"At daybreak he departed and went into a deserted place." (Luke 4:42a) Jesus' prayer in solitude opened his heart to God's presence and spirit. It formed who he was as a person. His intimate relationship

with God made him a complete and authentic human being. His intimacy with God became the source of all his words and action and determined his relationships with other people. His experience of God in prayer became the way he viewed and understood life. At the same time, his personal prayer took place in the wider context of his Jewish heritage, liturgical life, and his knowledge and understanding of Jewish sacred scriptures. This formative background gave birth to his compassionate engagement in the needs of his society.

Jesus, in his life of prayer, gives an example of how to listen to another voice. He lived a contemplative life and invites persons who follow him to a disciplined pattern of listening to God. Jesus demonstrated that when a person listens to God through some form of meditation she or he will be able to hear that same voice in all venues of life. And it's not a loud or coercive voice, even when it challenges a person to some form of action. Jesus demonstrated that the life of God is always within us, waiting for us.

Jesus' life of prayer provides a unique example of what God desires for human life.

The evolution of Christness as a way of life

Perhaps the best way to describe Christness is to narrate my own experience of Christness. I have discovered that Christness is a reality to be accepted and not a theory or discipline to be mastered. My journey into Christness began by learning about the life of Jesus of Nazareth rather than a focus on theology about Jesus. I relied on the gospels of Matthew, Mark, Luke and John. I was influenced, also, by the lives and witness of Jesus' earliest followers after his resurrection recorded in the New Testament book of Acts and epistles.

Eventually, I realized that my access to the gospels and epistles was part of a living tradition that extends into the lives of modern followers of Jesus. As I consciously became part of the life of a community of Jesus' followers I discovered that the life of Jesus is not a "past" life. Many persons in several differing

Christian faith communities shared their own experiences of Jesus' continuing life through worship—especially the Eucharist (Holy Communion), fellowship, learning and personal involvement in the lives of other people.

I'm not sure when I, too, wanted to be a follower of Jesus. The more his life became real in a variety of ways, the more I was attracted to him. Eventually I wanted to be like him. All this did not happen right away or with a single emotional "rush." In fact, after more than seventy years, I'm still learning what following Jesus means. Somehow, when I became open to the possibility of being like Jesus I began to learn, unconsciously, that I was not in complete control of the outcome.

As I look back on my life I can see how I was being formed, gradually, into Christness without really knowing what was happening or having Christness as an objective goal. Most of the time I have learned about following Jesus by working with and observing persons whose lives, in small and larger ways, were congruent with the life of Jesus. I could see him in their lives. They became my mentors, although I was not always aware of what was happening.

Over the years, with these really fine mentors, I have learned that if my ultimate goal in life is to follow Jesus for the good of all, then I must, with God's help, become a manifestation of Jesus' presence in the world. For this to become an authentic reality in my life I must, like Jesus, develop a solitary and contemplative experience of God that will guide and empower the incarnation of God in my daily life. Although this is not unique for me, it will make it possible for my one life to collaborate with God's desires for the life of the world. The path toward Christness is a combination of my own desires and behavior collaborating with the gifts of God's spirit and grace-filled energy. It may begin with my desire and include continued effort on my part, but God will complete and sustain the manifestation of Jesus' life in me. As we have seen, in the words of St. Paul, who at one time persecuted followers of Jesus, *"It is no longer I who live, but Christ who lives in me."*

This will not happen overnight. I will be continually formed and sustained through my active life in a community of other followers of Jesus. Common work, study, and prayer will be the foundation of this environment of grace. The primary vocation of every Christian community is the transmission of experience of Jesus in such a way that he becomes tangible in the lives of its members as they make God's desires for the common good a reality.

"For the things which belong to the story of Jesus are not yet completed."[15]

This chapter has been one person's description of why Jesus' story gives fundamental meaning and purpose to a human life. But do not take my word for it. Decide for yourself. Jesus' primary way of teaching was the way he lived. He had an open and hospitable soul. His life was his message. What was that life like? The four New Testament gospels will help you see for yourself. *Reconsidering Jesus of Nazareth* will guide you through a brief summary of these gospels. I invite you to encounter Jesus in chapters two and three and decide whether his life of prayer and ministry are worthwhile.

Chapter 2

Jesus' Early Life

The four gospels tell very little about Jesus' early life. Matthew and Luke record the events surrounding the birth of Jesus.[16] Both accounts begin by emphasizing the significance of the life of the person their gospels proclaim. Their content includes literary forms of earlier oral tradition based on eyewitness accounts of Jesus' life and teaching as well as narratives influenced by the experiences and needs of Jesus' disciples after his resurrection.

The gospel of Matthew sets Jesus' birth in the context of his Jewish heritage linking him to Abraham, revered as the father of ancient Israel, and King David, idealized as Israel's most successful ruler[17]. This places him in a lineage that authenticates Jesus as the Messiah, the one anointed by God's Spirit who will fulfill the promises made by God to Abraham to make Israel a great nation through whom "all the families of the earth shall be blessed." (Gen 12:3) Matthew continues with details surrounding the birth of Jesus. Mary "was found to be with child from the Holy Spirit" while she is still engaged to Joseph—who could have disowned her. In a dream Joseph is told that Mary's child is "from the Holy Spirit" and that he is to be named "Jesus" because he will reconcile people to God. Joseph takes Mary as his wife and Jesus is born in Bethlehem.

Matthew's narrative continues with a visit from wise men from the East who—most likely using their knowledge of the stars and constellations and the history of eastern kingdoms—discern that a king will be born in Israel. They set out on a long journey and arrive in Jerusalem and ask King Herod the Great where this child—who is to be king of the Jews—has been born. They are directed to Bethlehem and offer the child exotic gifts to honor his birth. Then, realizing that Herod will want to kill a child who eventually will take over his throne, the wise men return home without telling Herod where they found the child. Herod is enraged and sends troops to kill all male children under the age of two in and around Bethlehem. After the wise men leave, Joseph is told in a dream to take Mary and Jesus and flee to Egypt until Herod dies. Mary, Joseph, and Jesus become refugees. When Herod the Great dies they return to Israel, but fearing Herod's son Archelaus in Judea, Joseph decides to settle to the north in Galilee in the town of Nazareth. Matthew's narrative then shifts from Jesus' infancy to Jesus adulthood and his baptism by John the Baptist in the Jordan River southeast of Jerusalem.

The gospel of Luke's narrative of Jesus' birth is quite different. (There are quite a few differences between similar narratives in the four gospels. This does not infer that only one gospel "got it right." Each evangelist has his own perspective and their sources from oral tradition vary at times. Each narrative conveys meaning about what happened and our task is to discern why each narrative is significant.) Luke adds details that Matthew omits, yet like Matthew, Luke's description of events surrounding Jesus' birth and early life continues to link Jesus to King David and Israel's hope for a messiah who will restore Israel to its Davidic influence and glory.[18] In chapter 4 Luke relates Jesus' adult activities to a "servant" mentioned in the prophet Isaiah who will bring "justice to the nations."[19] Luke begins his narrative with unusual events surrounding the birth of John the Baptist that foretell his adult ministry that will turn "many people of Israel to the Lord their God" and "make ready a people prepared for the Lord." Later we will see that John will influence the beginning of Jesus' adult ministry.

Luke continues with a visit of the angel Gabriel to Mary who proclaims that she is "favored by God" and will conceive and bear a son through the "power of the Most High."[20] He will be given the "throne of David" and his kingdom will have no end. Mary ponders this most unusual pronouncement and then gives her assent. When Mary becomes pregnant Luke narrates a visit by Mary to her relative Elizabeth who is pregnant with John (who as an adult will be called "the Baptist"). When Mary arrives, Elizabeth feels the child in her womb leap for joy and Mary responds with a song of praise that mirrors a similar song of praise by Hannah centuries earlier in thanksgiving for her child, Samuel, who became one of the greatest prophets in Israel. (Luke 1:46–55 and 1 Samuel 2:1–10) These narratives underline Luke's desire to connect Jesus with the throne of David, the prophets of Israel, and the activity of God's Spirit in Mary's pregnancy.

Luke then describes the birth of John the Baptist and includes a spirit-filled prophecy by John's father, the priest Zachariah, where—anticipating the ministries of John and Jesus—he proclaims "And you child, will be called the prophet of the Most High; for you will go before the Lord to prepare his ways, to give knowledge of salvation to his people by the forgiveness of their sins." (Luke 1:76–77)

Luke continues with the birth of Jesus, his naming at the time of his circumcision—eight days after his birth—and his presentation to God in the Jerusalem temple, since he was Mary's firstborn male child. It is significant that Luke places the birth in Bethlehem, linking Jesus to the house and family of King David and at the same time describes that shepherds are the first persons to know about Jesus' birth. Shepherds played an essential role in Jewish society. They had to be hearty, living outdoors, away from settlements and dedicated to caring for sheep that provided meat and wool. It was not an easy job. In the Hebrew scriptures shepherds were sometimes used as a symbols for Israel's leaders, appointed by God to care for the people. God was known as the "Shepherd of Israel." But some shepherds were held in low esteem because they were not always at home protecting their wives and children. Others were treated with suspicion because they grazed their flocks on other people's land. They were a marginal part of society. Luke—being aware the role of shepherds in Jewish society and of Jesus' adult ministry to marginalized people—seems eager to declare that shepherds are the first to know about Jesus' birth and that this child is the Messiah.

Luke's inclusion of Jesus' "naming" as well as his presentation to the Lord in the Temple demonstrates that Mary and Joseph follow the instructions of the angel Gabriel and name him "Jesus." These two events indicate, as well, that Mary and Joseph are devout Jews who comply with the requirements of the Torah to have Jesus circumcised—a physical sign of a male Jew's identity as a son of the Covenant made between the tribes of Israel and God at Mt. Sinai at the time of Moses. As Mary's first son, Jesus is to be offered and presented to the Lord. At the presentation of Jesus an unusual and important incident takes place in the Temple. Luke tells that an old man, Simeon, had been assured by the Holy Spirit that he would not die until he had seen "the Lord's Messiah." Guided by the Spirit he goes to the Temple and when he sees the infant Jesus he takes him into his arms and praises God, indicating that he can now die in peace "…for mine eyes have seen your salvation…a light for revelation to the Gentiles and for the glory of your people Israel." (Luke 2:30–32) Mary and Joseph are amazed at Simeon's actions and words. In addition, an elderly prophet, Anna, who prayed constantly at the Temple began "…to speak about the child to all who were looking for the redemption of Jerusalem." (Luke 2:38)

Luke's final narrative in Jesus' early life takes place after Mary and Joseph have moved to Nazareth when Jesus is twelve years old. Once again Luke is intent on showing that Jesus' parents are devout first-century Jews. He begins by saying that they travel to Jerusalem every year for the festival of Passover. This time, however, Jesus remains in Jerusalem after his parents have left with other relatives for the journey home north to Nazareth in Galilee. They return to the Temple area and find Jesus "…sitting among the teachers, listening to them, and asking them questions. And all who heard him were amazed at his understanding and questions." (Luke 2:46–47) Mary and Joseph are "astonished" when they find their precocious son with the rabbis. Yet Jesus feels at home among the teachers and his mind is focused on them and not his family. At twelve years he is now required as a male Jew to say all the daily prayers he learned from Joseph and having studied the Torah, especially the prophets and psalms, in Nazareth perhaps he had a longing to learn more in Jerusalem. He returns home with his parents and Mary ponders this incident along with the other events that began with the visit from the angel Gabriel.

All these incidents are included to demonstrate the significance of the remainder of Luke's gospel and in Luke's words to show that Jesus "…increased in wisdom and in years, and in divine and human favor." (Luke 2:52) Then Luke, in chapter 3, moves from Jesus' adolescence to the ministry of John the Baptist and Jesus' baptism as an adult.

The gospels of Mark and John include nothing about Jesus' birth and early years, although John begins his gospel with a poetic statement about the divine nature of Jesus as the Word of God—the source of all creation—and declares that "…the Word became flesh and lived among us, and we have seen his glory, the glory of a father's only son, full of grace and truth." (John 1:14) After this introduction, John describes Jesus' baptism, the relationship and ministries of Jesus and John the Baptist, and the beginning of Jesus' ministry announcing that the reign of God has begun and is tangible in people's lives through Jesus' activities.

Mark begins with a brief, yet bold, statement about the main character in his gospel: "*The beginning of the good news of Jesus Christ,* ["the anointed one"] *the Son of God.*" He is very clear about the significance of Jesus and relates his relationship with John the Baptist to a proclamation in the ancient Hebrew scriptures by the prophet Isaiah: "*See, I am sending my messenger ahead of you, who will prepare the way; the voice of one crying out in the wilderness: 'Prepare the way of the Lord, make his paths straight.'*" (Mark 1:1-3) Then Mark describes the ministry of John, Jesus' baptism, his temptations in the wilderness, and the beginning of his Galilean ministry.

The reign of God in Israel's history

To understand why Jesus' began his ministry with a proclamation that the "reign of God" was breaking in upon the people of Israel we must look briefly at Israel's history. What is "the reign of God" and why is it important? Like their ancestors, first-century Jews believed firmly that the God encountered by Abraham, Moses, and King David reigned over the entire world. "The Lord has established his throne in the heavens, and his kingdom rules over all." (Psalm 103:19) Although the images of "king" and "kingdom" are not held in high esteem in the twenty-first century, they were positive images in Jesus' heritage. The kingly reign of God conveyed the reality that God cares for, sustains, and protects Israel because of the covenant made at Mt. Sinai during the time of Moses. Justice and righteousness were the "pillars" of God's reign.[21] Later in Israel's history, King David formed the twelve tribes into a kingdom and made Jerusalem the religious and political center of its life. David extended the boundaries of Israel and his son, Solomon, built a temple in Jerusalem as a dwelling place for God's presence. Although both David and Solomon were complex and flawed human beings, they were also brilliant, faith-filled, and effective rulers. They were considered representatives of God and entrusted with the care of God's people. Although David became the image of the "ideal" king whose lineage and realm would last forever, most of Israel's subsequent kings "did what was evil in the sight of the Lord." Israel's prophets spoke out against lack of faith, injustice, and acquisition of wealth at the expense of the poor. Prophets like Isaiah, Jeremiah, and Micah constantly reminded rulers, priests, and wealthy landowners of how far they had strayed from Israel's covenant with God. They tried to keep the vision of Israel's identity alive. In the words of Micah, "…and what does the Lord require of you but to do justice, and to love kindness, and to walk humbly with your God?" (Micah 6:8)

Eventually the nation David had established was divided into two kingdoms and both kingdoms fell under control of first Assyria and then Babylon. This began almost five-hundred years when Israel was dominated by Persian, Greek, Syrian, and Roman occupiers. Except for a brief period from 163 BCE–63BCE when Israel revolted against the Syrian ruler Antiochus IV—who tried to eliminate Israelite culture and religious life—they did not experience self-rule. It was during this period that intense longing developed for the elimination of foreign rule and a restoration of Israel's kingdom with the return of "the Lord's Anointed." As we have seen, the term "messiah" refers to a person anointed with God's Spirit who will continue the lineage of King David.

In 63 BCE Israel was occupied and ruled by the Roman Empire. By the time of Jesus' birth Herod the Great and—following his death in 4 BCE—his sons ruled Israel under Rome's authority and careful eye. Herod's family was part Jewish. Although he was viciously defensive of his local power, Herod rebuilt the Temple in Jerusalem and under Herodian rule Jewish religious life was encouraged, but always with an eye not to disturb Rome's desire for control. The challenge was peaceful coexistence. The Jerusalem Temple priests—whose High Priest was appointed by Rome—favored concessions to Roman authority to ensure continuation of Jewish religious life. A group called Pharisees—a lay movement of devout Jews—developed interpretations of the Torah to ensure that the integrity of Jewish life would not be undermined by the growing influence of Roman culture and religion. In addition, just before and during Jesus' lifetime, there were several violent uprisings against Rome led by self-proclaimed zealot Jewish leaders. Rome responded in force and crucified thousands of Jewish males. In response to one uprising in Sepphoris—when Jesus was a youth and only four miles from his home in Nazareth—Herod Antipas destroyed the city, crucified scores of Jewish men, and later rebuilt the city as his Galilean capitol.

This background is important for understanding the context for Israel's continuing expectation of God's intervention to restore their nation through a leader anointed by God: the Messiah. This explains why the four gospels set Jesus' birth and life within this background and provides insights for the ministries of John the Baptist and Jesus.

Chapter 3

Jesus' Ministry

The activity of John the Baptist and Jesus' proclamation of the reign of God

Sometime in early 28 CE John, who would become known as "the baptizer," left his small village within walking distance of Jerusalem.[22] His father, Zechariah was a priest of the Temple, but John was dissatisfied with Temple worship and his faith community's lack of commitment to the covenant Israel had made with God at the time of Moses. He went to an area east of the Jordan River and began preaching a message that the people of Israel were at a threshold in their life with God. Their lives were no longer congruent with what their acceptance of the Torah required. When John and Jesus spoke of "sinners," and "sinners" are mentioned in the book of Acts and the letters of St. Paul, the meaning refers to persons who have either rejected or, by their behavior, have departed from fulfilling the Torah. Since the Torah is the path toward life, they have rejected the life God offers and the blessing (life force for the soul) God desires to give each person. Worship and claiming the inheritance of the promises God made to Abraham could not justify or redeem the evil present in their lives. The gospels in varying narratives place John's demeanor and message, as well as his persona and dress, in the tradition of Israel's prophets. John's message is simple, yet profound and requires a response from every person who hears his voice: *the people of Israel have betrayed their covenanted relationship with God and God is now moving in their midst to renew his people. Each person must repent—turn toward God—and renew their relationship with God.* John offered a cleansing through immersion in the Jordan River as a sign of a person's repentance and commitment to embrace a renewed way of life. He was firm in his belief that this was a matter of life and death; people would suffer the consequences of maintaining their sinful lives. John was very clear that God's reign was breaking into the lives of the people of Israel.

At the same time, John realized that he was not the person who would renew Israel. There is someone coming after him. "Among you stands one whom you do not know, the one who is coming after me…" (John 1:26–27a) "I baptize you with water; but one who is more powerful than I is coming; I am not worthy to untie the thong of his sandals. He will baptize you with the Holy Spirit and with fire." (Luke 3:16)

The baptism of Jesus

It is in this context that Jesus travels from Galilee to the area where John is baptizing. It is clear that Jesus was moved by what he had heard of John and wanted to experience his activities first-hand. Shortly after his arrival he is baptized by John in the Jordan River. As Jesus is praying in the river he experiences the presence of God in a way that will transform his life and makes him aware that he has a unique and filial intimacy with God whom he will call "Abba" from that time forward. His mystical experience is described by Matthew, Mark, and Luke using typical Middle Eastern images. The "heavens open" and Jesus experiences God's presence tangibly. The Spirit descends in the form of a dove—the symbol of intimacy—and a voice "from heaven" declares "…You are my Son, the Beloved; with you I am well pleased." (Luke 3:22) The author of John's gospel narrates John the Baptist's testimony describing the significance of Jesus' baptism: "I saw the Spirit descending from heaven like a dove, and it remained on him. I myself did not know him, but the one who sent me to baptize with water said to me, 'He on whom you see the Spirit descend and remain is the one who baptizes with the Holy Spirit.' And I myself have seen and have testified that this is the Son of God." (John 1:32–34) This testimony is congruent with the manner in which the Spirit of God "rested" on the shoulders and in the lives of Israel's prophets. They were anointed by the Spirit. During the century before the birth of Jesus Jewish wisdom literature spoke of the coming of "the Lord's Anointed."

Most New Testament scholars agree that Jesus' acceptance of John's baptism was his way of affirming John's basic message: God was acting in the lives of the people of Israel to renew their relationship with God. But it was not enough to agree with the message. Each person must respond to the message and, through baptism, enter into a changed way of life. The movement of God's Spirit uncovers sinfulness and faithlessness. This awareness prompts a life and death decision to enter into a renewed relationship with God. It is the palpable presence of God at this time in Israel's life that offers the challenge for each person to "repent"—turn around—and embrace the reign of God. John is very clear that persons who reject God's challenge will be under God's judgment, yet he also offers advice about human relationships that will fulfill God's desires for human life. (see Luke 3:10–14)

Space does not permit more details about the relationship between John the Baptist and Jesus. The gospels leave little doubt that Jesus was influenced significantly by his kinsman John and shared John's passionate belief that God was "breaking into" the lives of the people of Israel. It is clear, also, that at some point Jesus parted company with John and began his own proclamation of the need for repentance and commitment to the reign of God. Unlike John, whose ministry was centered in one place, Jesus will take the news of the immanent reign of God throughout Israel.

Jesus' temptations in the wilderness

Luke describes what happened soon after Jesus' baptism. "Jesus, full of the Holy Spirit, left the area where he was baptized and was led by the Spirit to a wilderness, where for forty days he was tempted by the devil." (Luke 4:1–2) The baptism was, indeed, an anointing with the Spirit who now leads Jesus into the desert where he is "tested" by a diabolic figure called Satan or "the devil." In the Greek text of Luke, this figure is called "diabolou," the one who scatters. In the Hebrew Scriptures Satan is a mysterious figure whose purpose is to scatter a person's commitment to God. "A 'temptation' means a trial or opportunity to prove one's self, rather than a seduction to wrong doing."[23] In the wilderness Jesus experiences three tests that help him discern how he is to live out the unique relationship with God that was revealed to him at his baptism. How is he to use the presence of God's power in his life? Can he invoke God to do his will or is it the other way around? (i.e. "Who is in charge?") What is most fundamental in this filial relationship with God? In all three tests Jesus discerns what God desires through his substantive knowledge and reflection on the Hebrew Scriptures. Each time Satan offers something Jesus replies with "It is written, it is written, it is written." Jesus is rooted in his Jewish spiritual heritage and discerns that his relationship with his Abba must be congruent with what God desires and with God's activity in Israel at the present time.

The Beginning of Jesus' good news about the reign of God

Luke tells us that Jesus left the wilderness and returned to Galilee. "Then Jesus, filled with the power of the Spirit, returned to Galilee, and a report about him spread through all the surrounding country. He began to teach in their synagogues and was praised by everyone." (Luke 4:14–15) Mark summarizes the content of his message: "…The time is fulfilled, and the kingdom of God has come near; repent, and believe in the good news." (Mark 1:14) This is Jesus' "gospel."

Jesus baptism and temptations in the wilderness have made him acutely aware that the reign of God is "rushing into" the lives of the people of Israel and will be manifested through his words and actions. All four gospels narrate his compassionate engagement in people's lives.

Here are a few examples:

- He worships and preaches in the synagogue in Nazareth. He mirrors the words of the prophet Isaiah: "The Spirit of the Lord is upon me, because he has anointed me to bring good news to the poor…" (Luke 4:16–21)

He worships in the Capernaum synagogue, heals a man possessed with a demon, and heals Peter's mother-in-law. (Luke 4:31–38)

- The next day, after he had been praying in a deserted place early in the morning, crowds found him and wanted to keep him from leaving Capernaum, but Jesus said "I must go to the other towns and declare the good news of the reign of God, for I was sent for this purpose." He then preached in synagogues throughout Judea. (Luke 4:42–44)

- Travelling near the village of Nain, Jesus restores the son of a widow to life and in doing so restores the widow's place in her family and community. (Luke 7:11–17)

- Jesus casts out demons in a variety of places and situations. (Matthew 17:14–20; Mark 1:21–28)

- He heals lepers and a woman with an issue of blood. (Mark1:40–45; Luke 17:11–19; 5:24b–34)

- He heals a centurion's servant. (Matthew 8:5–13)

How can the reign of God be recognized? When is it "here"?

Jesus used many images, usually parables, to describe the presence of God's reign. Here are two examples directed to those closest to him as they walked throughout Galilee:

"Blessed are your eyes, for they see, and your ears, for they hear. Truly, I say to you, many prophets and righteous men longed to see

what you see, and did not see it, and to hear what you hear, and did not hear it." (Matthew 13:16–17)

In another context, possibly when a group of Jesus' disciples returned from a healing and preaching mission and said, *"Lord, even the demons are subject to us in your name!"*, Jesus replies: *"I was watching Satan fall like the lightening from heaven!"* Then Jesus adds: *"To you it has been given to know the mysteries of God, but for others they are in parables so that seeing they may not see, and hearing they may not hear."* (Luke 10:17–24)

What is going on here?

Jesus is making it clear that the "Kingdom of Heaven," the reign of God, is not an abstract or philosophical concept or esoteric place. It is real and can be experienced in time and space by human senses and experience. At the same time a person must be able to see and discern the significance of the words and actions that are taking place before their ears and eyes. T.W. Manson, a New Testament scholar in the mid-twentieth-century, pointed out that "The blessedness consists not in the fact that their eyes are open, but that there is something to be seen by the open-eyed, the manifestation, namely, of the kingdom of God."

The Hebrews did not describe their awareness of God's presence primarily in theological statements or in wise sayings. Their wisdom was simple and practical. They experienced God in the mundane events of daily life as well as unique and extraordinary events. They were able to "see into" what was happening before their eyes and the the meaning of these experiences almost always elicited a response. Commenting on the miracle of the parting of the Red Sea Rabbi Eliezer (a contemporary of Jesus in the first century) said: *"How does one know that at the Red Sea even the maidservants saw what Isaiah and Ezekiel never were fortunate enough to see? Because Scripture says about them, 'And through the prophets I gave parables.'"* [24] David Biven, a modern scholar of the life of Jesus in his own Jewish culture says that *"God did not reveal himself even to the prophets in the same mighty way that he did to the whole people, great and small, at the Red Sea. What did these humble servant girls see? They witnessed a great demonstration of God's power, the dividing of the Red Sea. They saw God's kingdom."[25]*

A powerful example of Jesus' declaration that the reign of God is present in his words and actions is in his reply to the disciples of John the Baptizer. John is no longer certain that Jesus is the agent of God who is to come to establish the reign of God and sends disciples to Jesus. They ask: *"Are you the Coming One?"* Jesus' reply is simple: *Report to John what you have seen and heard."* (Luke 7:18–23) Jesus was aware that in his healings, bringing the dead to life, feeding the hungry, forgiving sinners, and in his teaching people had the opportunity to see and hear the reign of God in their midst. (Luke 7:36–50; 6: 20–42; John 8:1–11)

But Jesus was aware, also, that just being present or listening to words is not enough. A person had to be open to God's presence, to let go of control of what he or she wanted to see or hear or already believed or knew. That is why he said that he spoke in parables so that they would hear, but not understand, and see and not comprehend. The self-righteous and self-assured will not see or hear what they, themselves, refuse to hear and see. (Matthew 10:13–17)

Once again, Jesus points to the need for an attitude of listening and discernment; he knows that intimacy with God enables a person to see God and hear God in everyday life when they have first seen and heard God within their heart in prayer. (Matthew 13:16–17) He knows this from his own experience.

How did Jesus and his disciples embody the reign of God?

It is essential to remember that Jesus was a devout Jew and was faithful to his religious tradition. His embodiment of the reign of God was not an attempt to begin a new religion. His passion was to demonstrate that through his life God was initiating a renewal and reorientation of his Jewish world. He saw that radical changes in the lives of people, their leaders, and their society would bring God's reign—that was already near—into manifestation.

Jesus' embodied the reign of God through an experiential and dynamic "movement" that was outside the norms of first century family relationships and responsibilities and was not sanctioned by the religious institutions and authorities of his day.

- He did not depend on normal family resources and support.
- He was challenged to justify the authority of his actions and teachings.
- He demanded a personal decision to become involved in his transformative movement
- He had to manifest the reign of God in the midst of constant doubts, clashes, and discussion regarding the validity of his words and actions.
- His itinerant movement and the numbers of disciples and other temporary followers posed challenges when visiting homes and villages because normal family and village life was disrupted.
- The implementation of Jesus' movement was neither convenient nor conventional; his inclusion of women and children who travelled with him was shocking to some of his critics.
- The movement included access to and relationships with persons who were considered unclean, sinners, and marginalized by conventional society; the movement crossed many boundaries, including the boundary between what the Torah and its interpreters declared was "clean" and "unclean." A person who was declared unclean could no longer worship with the community and was put on the margin of community life to protect those who were "clean."
- There was an urgency regarding time and place that kept Jesus moving from place to place on foot.

Jesus is convinced that his role in the manifestation of God's reign is unique and at the same time to be shared with his most intimate disciples. He authorizes and sends them to teach, heal, and cast out demons. He exhorts them to share the same intimacy with God that he experienced, as embodied in the "Lord's Prayer."

His movement (we might call it his mission) is held together by each disciple's relationship with Jesus. Jesus' disciples are a mixed group and share life together, but the "movement" is not sustained by the authority or power of the group; it is rooted and grounded in Jesus and his intimacy with God. The movement is God's doing and does not have a life apart from God. The disciples do not create the reign of God; they are called to enter where God reigns by manifesting God's desires in their lives. (This is why the disciples "fell apart" and left Jesus alone at the cross and after his death).

Jesus was the central figure in his movement and yet he balanced time with the group with his silence and solitude. Although he was "in charge" from the disciple's point of view, his words and power were not his own; they were manifestations of his Abba who sent him.

People around Jesus are attracted to him because they discern the possibility for their lives to change. Something happens to them when they are with him and they are changed by his words and actions. The normal barriers within society disappear around him, especially for the sick, the poor, women, sinners, and children. They recognized and sought the power manifested in his life. Most of what we know about Jesus comes from the memories and reactions of the people attracted to him.

In the midst of people's desire for Jesus, his primary concern was to lead them to his Abba, not to him. The movement of Jesus had one primary purpose: to enable people to experience God's love and power. This experience restored their integrity and transformed their lives, but did not eliminate the powers, diseases, and dysfunctions of society that enslaved them. Jesus' movement was intent on removing all things, attitudes, desires, and relationships that prevented the imminent arrival of the reign of God. Jesus wanted his movement to be the instrument for the regeneration of his Jewish world and the restoration of relationships between people that would make God's reign a reality. This is why he emphasized honoring God's place in people's lives, the desires of God for human life, total dependence on God, forgiveness, and seeking God's help to avoid evil. Jesus was very clear that persons who want to follow him should embody these behaviors and pray for God's help to make them a reality. This is the heart of what has become known as "The Lord's Prayer." It is probably the most familiar part of all Jesus' teaching and the most difficult to live by. It is easy to say this prayer personally or in a worship service and then leave it behind as we get on with daily life. Yet Jesus was very clear: if a person wants to follow him, the words of the "Lord's Prayer" must be taken seriously as his Way of Life. It is not easy and requires honest self-knowledge and both a desire for forgiveness and a forgiving heart.

Jesus' movement was one of many movements in his day. Its primary purpose was to promote peace and well-being and, with God's power, to make them possible. The Jesus movement always included sharing food and meals with a variety of people. Many of Jesus' parables describing the reign of God are set in the context of meals and banquets. Jesus' willingness to share food with unacceptable persons was the source of significant criticism and at the same time was a sign of the inclusiveness of God's reign. The image of a banquet was not only a present sign of God's reign, it was also used by Jesus as an image of a future banquet that would include persons from every nation and era of human history.

The heart of Jesus' teaching and actions about the reign of God was centered in the present. "The Kingdom is very near." Jesus sensed that God's activity in people's lives during his lifetime and, in fact, through his life itself, was a sign that the Kingdom was a present reality and not only a future hope. As we have seen in the previous paragraphs, the tangible characteristics of the reign of God as a present reality may be seen in the "Lord's Prayer." They are present, also, in a collection of Jesus' sayings called "The Beatitudes," a part of what has become known as "The Sermon on the Mount" in Matthew's gospel (Matthew 5–7) and the Sermon on the Plain in Luke's gospel (Luke 6:17–49). In these sayings Jesus describes a person's fundamental relationship with God and how that will empower the reign of God in that person's life.

The Sermon on the Mount

Jesus teaches that becoming his disciple will mean more than rearranging a few details in a person's spiritual life.

- What is prayer? (Matthew 6:5-8)

    a. It is an attitude in our relationship with God (5-6)

    b. The heart of prayer is an authentic relationship with God that fills life with meaning. Prayer links our attitude about life with God's attitude and desires for life. (7-8) Our experience of God in prayer flows into our lives as love of God and our neighbor.

- Prayer is directly related to and embodied in our actions in daily life. It begins in the heart and flows from there into our actions. The motivation for prayer determines its authenticity. (Matthew 6:7–24)

    a. Jesus mirrors the teachings of the Hebrew prophets: (1 Samuel 15:22-23), words directed to King Saul, (Isaiah 1:10-14), God's frustration with empty prayer and liturgies, (Jeremiah 7:21-24), worship without commitment to God is worthless, (Hosea 6:6), God desires genuine love and experience of God, not empty offerings, (Micah 6:6-8), prayer and action must be congruent and aligns our desires with God's desires. Prayer is a call to action.

    b. Jesus went out to the mountain to pray and he prayed to God all night. At daybreak, motivated by his experience of God in prayer, he gathers his disciples and chooses twelve; then he takes the twelve down the mountain. The people came to him to "hear" him and be healed; "The whole crowd wanted to touch him because power was going out of him and he was healing everyone." (Luke 6:12–19)

Then Jesus describes what life is like in the "kingdom of God."

"Woe to the shepherds who destroy and scatter the sheep of my pasture! says the Lord. Therefore thus says the Lord, the God of Israel, concerning the shepherds who shepherd my people. It is you who have scattered my flock, and have driven them away, and you have

not attended to them…I will raise up shepherds over them who will shepherd them, and they shall not fear any longer, or be dismayed, nor shall any be missing, says the Lord." (Jeremiah 23:1–2; 4)

In the Beatitudes (Matthew 5:1–11) Jesus outlines the characteristics of faithful shepherds in the reign of God and ways that God's reign will change and bring hope to the lives of a variety of people. The Beatitudes are not abstract wisdom sayings. They are a call to participate in the reign of God and a promise of what will await each person who responds.[26] The reign of God is not for spectators. And it begins in the lives of persons who have the greatest needs.

Jesus begins each portrayal with *"Blessed are…"* In my book *Lord, Teach Us To Pray: One Hundred Daily Reflections on Jesus' Life of Prayer"* I describe the significance of "blessing" in Jesus' culture as follows:

"In Hebrew culture a 'blessing' is the sharing of power (the life force) from one soul to another. That blessing can make each soul prosper as it fulfills its purpose in the world God has made. The soul of each person will only experience peace (fulfill its purpose) when it is in harmony with all other souls who are committed to the same covenant. The power that makes this possible, the *'berakha'* (blessing), acts within the soul yet cannot be separated from its outward manifestation in the life of a person. One who is blessed will radiate the power of that blessing. Blessing, then, is the source of righteousness, justice, and peace. Happiness is living in the fruits of blessing. 'Tell the innocent how fortunate they are; for they shall eat the fruit of their labors.' (Isaiah 3:10)"[27]

"It is with this deeply rooted Hebrew awareness of blessing that Jesus exhorts his disciples to be "pure in spirit" (humble), …"meek" (not self-serving), …to *"hunger and thirst for righteousness"* (work tirelessly for the common good), …be *"merciful"* (have patience and solidarity with others),… seek *"purity of heart"* (single-minded openness to God and others),… become *"peacemakers"* (persons who share a blessing), …and trust in the ability to withstand persecution and marginalization for the sake of the reign of God.

"All this is framed by the *honor/shame* foundation of Jesus' society. To be blessed is to be held honorable in the sight of God. These characteristics may be called 'prayer-in-action'. They make the inner life of the soul tangible in daily life. They were the fruits of Jesus' prayer."[28]

The chronology of Jesus' world view had three parts[29]:

- The biblical age that began with Abraham and ended with John the Baptist
- The period during Jesus' lifetime when the reign of God was rushing into the life of the people of Israel
- A future judgment with the Son of Man as Judge, followed by resurrection, and the beginning of the age to come and eternal life

Jesus had a new and creative interpretation of God's desires for God's reign. This seems to have been a direct result of *his life of prayer and contemplative listening to his Abba.* Modern scholars do not give this dimension of Jesus' life the credit it deserves. It is essential to discover this source of Jesus' innovative understanding of his role in the inauguration of the reign of God and the nature of the reign, itself.

The evangelists narrate a clear pattern in Jesus' daily life where he goes off to a variety of "deserts" throughout his three-year mission. His time in the desert after his baptism was just the beginning of a constant discipline of intimacy and listening to God. This time *was the source of his power, wisdom, and courage as a seer, sage, and guide for disciples.* Jesus' quiet listening and faithful discernment was the source of his deep inner understanding of the reign of God that he shared with his disciples and embodied through his compassionate engagement in first-century Jewish society.

Jesus was convinced that the wisdom and understanding of the mysteries of God, God's reign, and God's involvement in history was not the exclusive intellectual property of the well-educated and powerful who can afford education and have time for leisure to study and ponder. Jesus, through his teaching to crowds and the inner group of his disciples, demonstrated that God's wisdom is not the exclusive domain of the upper classes and religious leaders of his day. His teaching methods show that this wisdom *should be mediated and made available to the poor, uneducated, and ordinary people* through the ordinary and every-day circumstances of their lives in families and village life. (Matthew 11:25–30 and Luke 10:21)

Like many teachers in his day, Jesus used parables. A parable uses an incident or situation that is already familiar to its hearers to get their attention and lead them to ponder its content. Parables usually have only one point. It is tempting today to relate them to a variety of situations or impose several meanings on them. But we should look for Jesus' meaning and remember that his parables were meant for people in his culture. Once we see his original meaning, then we can relate a parable to our lives today. One of Jesus' best known parables is called "The Prodigal Son." (Luke 15:11–32) It should be called "The Forgiving Father" because Jesus is describing the nature of God's unconditional love for a person and God's willingness to forgive. Sometimes Jesus would use extreme exaggeration to get hearers' attention or to prompt people to think about something they would prefer to avoid. *"If your eye causes you to sin, tear it out and throw it away; it is better for you to lose one of your members than for your whole body to be thrown into hell."* (Matthew 5:29) Jesus is pointing to a person's ability to rationalize the seriousness of sexual desires that can lead to infidelity and will damage and alienate the lives of all concerned. He is saying "tear yourself away from unrestrained pleasure that will infect your whole life."

Chapter 4

Jesus' Stewardship of Power

The Epistle for Palm Sunday, from St. Paul's Letter to the Colossians, makes a bold statement about Jesus of Nazareth. "For in him all the fullness of God was pleased to dwell..." (Colossians 1:19). If this is true, then every word and action of Jesus reveals what God is like.

Jesus washes his disciples' feet at "The Last Supper"

Matthew, Mark, and Luke describe Jesus celebrating a Passover meal with his disciples in Jerusalem on the night before he was crucified. (Matthew 26:17–30; Mark 14:12–25; Luke 22:1-23)[30] John's gospel places this meal just prior to the Passover. (John 13:1–20) John narrates an unusual event during the supper that took Jesus' disciples by surprise.

"Jesus, knowing that the Father had given all things into his hands, and that he had come from God and was going to God, got up from the table, took off his outer robe, and tied a towel around himself. Then he poured water into a basin and began to wash the disciples' feet and to wipe them with the towel that was tied around him." (John 13:3–5)

What do Jesus' words and actions in this narrative teach us about God? As happens so often in John's gospel, there is an inner meaning to Jesus' words and behavior. If we are, as St. Paul exhorts, to "put on the mind of Christ" and become Christ's presence in the

48

world today, then the words and actions of Jesus during the "foot washing" also teach us about ourselves.

So what is happening in this foot washing narrative?

- During supper Jesus gets up and takes off his outer robe.

- He ties a towel around his waist, gets a basin of water, and begins to wash the disciples' feet.

- Peter recoils from the idea that Jesus wants to wash his feet. He says, "You will never wash my feet!"

- Jesus responds, "Unless I wash you, you have no share with me."

- Peter acknowledges his error and responds, "Lord not my feet only, but also my hands and my head."

- After the foot washing Jesus puts on his outer robe again and begins to speak: *"Do you know what I have done to you? You call me teacher and Lord —and you are right, for that is what I am. So if I, your Lord and Teacher, have washed your feet, you also should wash one another's feet. For I have set you an example, that you should do as I have done to you."* (John 13: 12b–15)

Jesus turns the conventional purpose of power upside down

The inner meaning of the foot washing incident is embedded in *the action of Jesus taking off his outer robe and his response to Peter's refusal to have Jesus wash his feet.* Let's look more closely.[31]

One traditional explanation of the foot washing is that it proclaims a core Christian virtue of hospitality. The foot washing is also interpreted as setting forth the Christian virtue of being a servant to other people. But these are not the primary messages behind Jesus' words or actions in the foot washing. There is a deeper issue at work in the foot washing narrative. Jesus' disciples were confused about his actions and this prompted Jesus to ask: *"Do you know what I have done to you?"* Removing his outer garment is one of two clues. Jesus was called "rabbi," a term used in the first century to show respect for an esteemed teacher. Even his opponents acknowledged him as a rabbi and a teacher of God's wisdom. Rabbis were respected teachers and interpreters of the Torah and had power to settle disputes. They were a combination of civil judge, seminary professor, and pastor. They had power; lots of power. (That is one reason why Jesus' opponents wanted to silence him.)

When Jesus takes off his outer garment he is making a radical statement about the nature and purpose of power. The one who is a powerful teacher and the founder of his movement chooses the role of a servant, washing the feet of those who have accepted his authority as a teacher and as a steward of their lives. In Jesus' culture the lord of a manor was the steward of the land and was expected to share his resources with the people who lived on and worked his land. Although he was the owner, he bore responsibility for the welfare of those who helped make his land bear fruit. A rabbi through his authority as teacher and civil judge was a steward of the public and spiritual lives of his disciples. So you can see why Jesus' disciples called him "Teacher and Lord."

John tells us that Jesus takes off his outer robe, ties a towel around his waist, pours water in a basin, and begins to wash the disciples' feet, drying them with the towel. These actions puzzle the disciples for two reasons. In Jesus' culture, only slaves or servants washed the feet of members of a household. It was unthinkable that Jesus, as their master and teacher, wants to wash their feet. In addition, feet and shoes (or sandals) were considered unclean. To show your shoe or foot to another person was considered an insult. The disciples of a rabbi followed him everywhere and served his basic needs, except for washing his feet. Jesus was doing something unthinkable. He is turning a cultural norm upside-down. He is removing the traditional boundaries between "teacher" and disciple and offering an intimate and life-giving relationship.

This is why Peter does not want Jesus to wash his feet. He prefers to live by the established boundaries between him and Jesus.[32] In Peter's mind, Jesus is above him because he is his teacher and Lord. The teacher should not be washing a disciple's feet. Peter wants to keep Jesus "in his place". And so, Peter uses the only power he can to try to coerce Jesus to remain a conventional teacher and Lord. Using preemptive force Peter issues an ultimatum: "You will never wash my feet!" Although Peter's motive is genuine respect for his Rabbi and Lord, he refuses to accept Jesus' behavior as one who serves. *He rejects both the actions of Jesus and the message they convey.* Peter tries to use raw power to control Jesus' behavior. He wants to determine who and what Jesus should be, so he tries to bully Jesus into conformity to Peter's vision of acceptable rabbinic behavior.

Jesus' response to Peter is swift, yet compassionate. Without judging Peter, Jesus points out the consequences of Peter's ultimatum: *"Unless I wash you, you have no share with me."* This bold statement relates to another norm in Jesus' culture. If a person offers you a gift or an opportunity, you honor the gift and the person by accepting what is offered. The giving and the response create a bond. The recipient is invited into communion with the giver. If Peter refuses Jesus' offer he is letting go of his relationship with Jesus as teacher as well as the presence of God in what Jesus is doing as a teacher.

Jesus dialogue with Peter provides a second clue to the inner meaning of the foot washing. Jesus wants the dialogue with Peter to continue, yet he continues to re-define the role of a rabbi. He is a rabbi, a teacher and leader, *who declares that the purpose of his power is to serve his disciples.* This was an unbelievably radical statement. Jesus' words and behavior contradicted the conventional wisdom of his day, even though they were congruent with the spiritual wisdom of his Jewish heritage. Jesus and his disciples lived in a country that was occupied by a foreign nation whose leaders "lorded it over their subjects". Jesus was aware that this pattern was present, also, in some of the spiritual and political leaders of his own people. His message to Peter and the other disciples is clear. His words mean "It should not be this way with you, if you are my disciples." Jesus, through his behavior, challenges his disciples to honor one another and serve the common good. Jesus actions are more powerful than his words.

It is essential to see that, in his response to Peter, Jesus practices what he preaches. *His message demonstrates that the gift of power is given to serve and bring life to others.* As a rabbi Jesus could have demanded Peter's compliance. He could have labeled Peter a dissenter and pushed him to the margins of Jesus' community. But his desire was that Peter would continue to "have a share with him". Jesus does not cut off dialogue with Peter because Peter disagrees with his actions. At the same time he lets Peter know the consequence of his ultimatum. "You will have no share with me." This is not a rejection of Peter. It is a warning, motivated by genuine concern, that Peter's desire to control Jesus will alienate him from who Jesus really is. Jesus was offering Peter, and the others present, the opportunity to become one with him, to share his life through a massive change of consciousness.

"Unless I wash you, you will have no share with me." Jesus is offering a form of baptism into a new world view of human relationships. This second clue in the foot washing points toward a crossing over, a paschal journey, from a world in which power is used for domination to a world in which power creates communion. He frames this exodus by reminding his disciples that relationships structured by self-centered possession of power (whether they are political, military, economic, or religious) always fragment society and are characterized by competition, comparison and exclusion. By taking off his rabbi's garment and washing the disciples' feet Jesus invites those present to enter relationships that are based on mutual respect, collaboration, and participation. (…not on "lording it over" other people).

Such a radical shift requires a change of consciousness, a total change in the way a person looks at the world and other people. Jesus experienced this change of consciousness because he was totally immersed in the life and love of God. His most passionate desire is to share this consciousness, and the life it makes possible, with his disciples. "I give you a new commandment: that you love one another." "I no longer call you servants…but I have called you my friends, because I have made known to you everything I have learned from my Abba, the Holy One."

Peter fought this shift of consciousness without really knowing what Jesus was offering him. "You will not wash *my* feet." When Jesus said "If I do not wash you, you will have no share with me." Peter suddenly left the wilderness of wanting to control his own life as well as that of his teacher and Lord and began the difficult journey into the reign of God. That is no easy exodus! As long as we are alive, the reign of God is to be lived here and now, not in the future. The present reign of God is the place where power is used to bring forth life. In this realm, institutional structures and powers are to be subordinate to and exist within what Jesus called "the reign or kingdom of God." In that reign, power exists to feed and make life possible, not to control and manipulate. The foot washing is a baptism into *the way of communion*. That is why the gospel of John sets this narrative in the context of a supper.

Peter may have been hot-headed; he was definitely a Type-A fisherman. But he was willing to admit his mistake and take the risk of letting go of control of his life. It must have come rushing into his consciousness like a forty-five foot wave into a beach. *"Lord, not my feet only, but also my hands and my head."*

When all had been washed, including Peter's "full-body" wash, Jesus posed a difficult question. In the context of Peter's negative judgment about Jesus' behavior, Jesus realized that everyone there was puzzled by and having a hard time accepting his radical actions. So he asks: "Do you know what I have done to you?"

Jesus asks this same question today. Yes, the foot washing is about hospitality and serving other people, but only in the context of the sacred gift of power. Hospitality is an exercise of the power of inclusiveness and sharing life's gifts. Jesus realized that the proper exercise of power requires a humble spirit and a flexible heart. Self-assertion and pre-emptive control transform power from a life-giving force into coercion. As we have seen, he turned the tables on those leaders in his country and faith community who used power to "lord it over others". *Jesus' actions in the foot washing offered a radical change of consciousness from the institutionalization of domination to an environment of communion.*

If Jesus was indeed the person in whom the fullness of God was truly present, what does his message in the foot washing narrative teach us about God?

If we are called to make Christ tangible in the world, what does the foot washing teach us about ourselves?

Jesus's vision of the reign of God: A place where power brings forth life

The reign of God[33] is first and foremost a way of living that manifests God's desires for human life. This means that justice and mercy are primary and that power is a sacred gift and responsibility to make this possible in tangible ways. The reign of God is at the same time an earthly and heavenly society where the primary relationship of every person is that person's relationship with God. Jesus makes this very clear through his own intimacy with his Abba. Everything he desired, said, and did came from his constant openness to and awareness of God's presence. He gave his total self and loyalty to this intimacy with God and insisted that his disciples follow his example. *He lived the reign of God more than he talked about it.* He began where God's love was most needed in the lives of persons who were sick, marginalized, and victims of greed and injustice.

As we have seen, Jesus was convinced that the reign of God was becoming a reality in and through his life. Its purpose was the restoration of Israel's life with God. Although the institutional life of his faith community was a source of formation and worship, it was not the focus of God's reign in Jesus' mind or actions. The focus of his life was in the lives of people and this is where the reign of God was being manifest.

Jesus did not call people to "church." He called them to compassionate engagement with each other's lives. This, he knew, would require total commitment and would begin locally with individual lives. The reign of God would not come overnight. It seems clear that Jesus never intended to "finish" or complete the reign of God during his lifetime. The most important task was, and remains, to make God's reign tangible in personal and specific ways with whatever efforts are possible. He told his disciples, *"You shall do greater things than I have done."* (John 14:12)

Jesus knew it would take time in the same way that it takes a mustard seed to grow into a large shrub. The key is to *begin with intimacy with God* that will transform and empower our lives. The way we live with other people will come forth from this intimacy with God. It requires total dependence on God. Living with God, depending totally on God, and making God's love tangible are the signs that the reign of God is present.

Chapter 5

Jesus' Passion for Life

Our search for meaning and purpose

You and I, consciously or unconsciously, ask basic questions about life. "Where have I come from?" "Who am I?" "What am I here for?" and "Where is my life going?" We seek meaning and purpose. We want our lives to be like walking a labyrinth, where the path leads to a center and not like a maze filled with dead ends. The meaning we seek is not a "head trip." We want to experience life, and if at all possible, have relationships and work that are fulfilling. It takes time to find our way. Sometimes mistakes or conditions beyond our control lead to dead ends where the passion and excitement for living evaporates.

Over forty years ago a friend of mine sent me a note written hastily on a torn piece of a paper bag. His life had met a dead end. His message hit me like a ton of bricks.

"Dave, if you find the time—please give me a list of some important lines out of the bible—perhaps lines that may help ease and give direction to a troubled/restless/anxious soul. I don't really know just how serious I am about Christ—but I do know about this reoccurring hell of an abyss, this dissatisfaction with life as I am now living it—this cycle of up-dull-down, it's hard and painful. But I don't want just a crutch to lean against troubled times! I want a solid deep felt purpose—a feeling/knowing of rightness to my life. An **active** peace and clearness."

I was stunned. I had no idea my friend was headed for this bottomless pit. My first impulse was to visit him. He was asking for companionship, not simply information. He was two hours away and by the time I called, his wife had found him unconscious after an attempt at suicide. He was committed to a psyche ward in a large hospital near my home. Over the next two months I visited him regularly and got permission to take him out on hour-long walks. In the midst of conversations we took many steps in silence; he was looking for some sign to confirm that he was worthwhile, that he was headed "somewhere." We did talk about biblical narratives, but not as proof texts to ensure a way out of his abyss. Gradually, thanks to a community of family, friends, and health care professionals his anxious soul was healed. He was able to glimpse some "rightness" and "clearness" about his life again. He and I did talk about "how serious" he was about Christ. I do not remember the details, but I wish my own understanding of Jesus' passion for life had been more mature and my knowledge of his ministry more informed as my friend and I pondered responses to his questions about Christ.

As I look back, perhaps what I have learned and experienced since then might have given my friend motivation to see the words, activities, and relationships in Jesus' life as inspiration for the renewal of his own life. I wish I could have shared the content of this chapter with him.

Jesus' passion for life

As we have seen in previous chapters, Jesus had a clear vision of the purpose and rightness of his life. The four gospels are filled with the details. Yet it is easy to overlook the passion present in these details. We usually reserve the word "passion" to describe the last week of Jesus' earthly life.

In Jesus' pilgrimage during Holy week we see a man…a human being. But we see more than a biological human being. We see a complete and authentic human being. We see the man, Jesus of Nazareth, passionately open to and filled with the spirit and nature of God. In the Christian liturgical year the observance of Holy Week often is consumed by a focus on Jesus' physical and emotional suffering before and during his crucifixion. We refer to that intense suffering as "Jesus' passion." But what brought Jesus to that "passion?" The passion of Holy Week was the consequence of another passion. Jesus was a man *passionate about life* and the need to be completely human, born of both flesh and the spirit.

The suffering during Holy Week was the consequence of Jesus' passion for life. He was passionate about uncovering the hypocrisy of religious and political leaders and the burdens they placed on ordinary people. He was willing to risk the consequence of his candor, his anger, and his protests. Jesus was passionate in his love and concern for victims, the ignorant, the spiritually apathetic, the poor, the marginalized, and the same religious and political leaders he criticized. Jesus was passionate about luring those around him into the compassionate and life-giving presence of God. Jesus was passionate about the reality of God's presence in life itself, in his own life, the lives of other people, and in the joys and tragedies within his own society.

It was this unrelenting passion for life that placed him in conflict with leaders in his society that abused their power and authority. His desire to recall them to authentic human life and restore justice and righteous living threatened their control of society. They chose to confront him and eliminate his influence. Eventually, Jesus realized that he must "go up to Jerusalem" and confront the abuses of his society at the seat of religious and political power. Jesus' simple entry into Jerusalem on a donkey was in stark contrast to the triumphal and controlling power of the Roman occupiers and to those leaders of his own faith community who used wealth and power to ensure their leadership and favor with Rome, in the name of protecting their religious traditions and practices. Jesus' passion in entering Jerusalem was not a suicidal mission to become a martyr for justice. At the same time he was clearly aware of the consequences of his teaching and protests in the seats of power. It was his passion for life that led both to the sufferings we label as his "passion" and to his death on the cross.

The vitality and spiritual power of Jesus' passion for life transcended his death. The same passion that was so vividly present during his life was present in his death and resurrection. It was that passion that filled the lives of those who experienced his risen presence. They, too, became passionate about life. They experienced God's life in Jesus so vividly that they eventually would call him God's son, Lord, and Savior. In the first century these titles were used, also, to refer to the Roman Emperor. The followers of Jesus were making a bold and courageous statement about his influence in their lives.

Each year during the months of Lent that precede Easter, we have the opportunity to enter a spirit of contemplation of Jesus' passion for life, to look anew at the four canonical gospels and discover that we, too, are called to be so open to God that we experience Jesus' oneness with God and his passion for life. In this way we will become fully and abundantly alive, authentically human, and capable of being a source of life to others. This passion for life will lead us in the same path Jesus followed, with the same consequences. We may experience pain and suffering. But we will also experience resurrection.

It is essential to see that Jesus' passion was manifested in *his entire life* and not only during his courageous suffering during what we call Holy Week. If we look at his passion for life throughout the canonical gospels we can see a three-fold pattern:

- Jesus was passionate about his relationship with his **Abba**, his heavenly father, the Holy One. He is passionate about this relationship and shows that it is what makes us children of God. Jesus' life of prayer included silent reflection in quiet places away from others, regular participation in synagogue worship and the great feasts at the Temple in Jerusalem, and in deep contemplative experience. (Luke describes Jesus at prayer "in God", not "to God".) Jesus was so committed to his life with God that he experienced a unity with God that enabled him to know that his words and actions came from God and not from his own wisdom and power. It was this union with God that enabled Jesus to manifest God's presence in his own life. St. Paul would say that in Jesus of Nazareth "... the fullness of God was pleased to dwell..." in human form. (Colossians 1:19) It was this non-dual relationship with God that was the source of Jesus compassion for all people and his delight in the sacredness of nature.

- Jesus' oneness with God enabled the presence of God to be manifest in his life. He was convinced that God's presence in his life was a "breaking-in" of God's reign (kingdom) into the lives of his people that would restore Israel to its original destiny. Jesus's greatest passion was for all those who were attracted to him to be one with the Father as he was one with the Father.(John 17:1–26) If we are passionate about our relationship with God, we will manifest God's presence in every aspect of our lives, including our homes. God will be revealed in us as God was revealed in Jesus. This is where family and home life begins. "In my Father's house there are many dwelling places." (John 14:2) The earliest Christian teachers were mystics and contemplatives. They believed, through their own experience, that we are called "to participate in the divine nature" (2 Peter 1:4).

- If we are passionate about our relationship with God and are truly open to God's presence in our lives, our lives will manifest God's presence. This union with God will evoke a *generative response* and will enter into every aspect of our daily lives. The world will be different because of our God-filled lives. And this living-presence, manifest in our words and actions, will evoke a similar generative response from others. This release of generativity is what gives life to the world and completes the creation of our humanness. In these ways we, too, will participate in God's reign in the world. Jesus said "I came that they may have life, and have it abundantly." (John 10:10) He was not talking about material security or abundance. He was speaking about the purity of heart, charity, and humility that are the womb of compassion, civility, and stewardship that enable us to know what is necessary for our lives and help us honor one another and serve the common good. This abundant life is impossible as long as we are in control of our own lives.

The passion of Jesus enables us to look at the life-pilgrimage of one man and see in his life a paradigm of our own life's pilgrimage. *Jesus did not die to somehow change God's mind about us...the death of Jesus can help us change our minds about ourselves.* The passion of Jesus can transform our lives...and the sad thing about his death is that he did not have to die to enable us to experience such transformation. Yet the passion for life that caused his death and resurrection draw us with amazing power to the transformation he makes possible. The reality of his death and resurrection became a powerful means for the *transmission* of his consciousness and unitive experience of God to us. St. Paul says it clearly: "So if anyone is in Christ, there is a new creation: everything old has passed away; see, everything has become new!" (2 Corinthians 5:17) That is the nature of sacred passion, whether at work, in society or in our homes. It transforms things and people; it draws out the best in others. It ennobles persons and events.

The passion of Jesus gives us an opportunity to look at and experience a man who was so fully alive and filled with God's spirit that our spirits will cry out to be that alive. It is this desire for aliveness and authenticity of life that releases us from those things that keep us from our full life with God and others, especially those closest to us in our homes and at work. The passion and energy of God's presence in Jesus can release whatever is within us that stands in the way of our intimacy with others at home and at work. Our western culture today is craving for this authentic intimacy. At the same time we are afraid of the mutual responsibilities and stewardship such intimacy will bring. We do not know how or where to find true intimacy and wholesome outlets for our passions. This is why our media, entertainment, and relationships are so dysfunctional. Only our naked presence to God's love will lure us to authentic human life; the passion of Jesus is a call to love.

This is what happened to those who experienced and were affected by Jesus' resurrection—once they had the courage to move beyond their discouragement about his death and their lost hopes. In the humanity and passion of Jesus those around him saw a sacrament of God—an outward and visible sign in his human life of the authentic presence of God—and Jesus called them to go beyond the sign of God in his life to *their own experience of God.* Jesus called those who were close to him, before and after his resurrection, to do greater things than he had done. (John 14:12) Jesus' passion was to transmit his enlightened experience of God to others. He knew that the consciousness of God present in his life was what God desires for every human being. He called people to discover the One who is already present in their lives. This is what he called living abundantly.

The pilgrimage of Jesus can draw us to what he desires for us: *our own pilgrimage into the heart of God.* The vitality and spiritual power of Jesus' passion transcended his death and the presence of God in the risen Christ transformed the lives of those who formed the earliest Christian faith communities. They, too, became passionate about life.

If we are passionate about our life with God our lives will manifest the wisdom, energy, consciousness, and presence of God. We will truly become sources of life for others…at home and at work. By sharing our passion we will not only be a source of life…we will lure others to discover the gift of God's passion in their lives. That is what Jesus meant when he exhorted his followers to pray that God's will be done on earth as it is in heaven.

Chapter 6

The Meaning of Jesus' Death

Introduction

In Chapter 5 we saw that Jesus' passion for life and his compassionate engagement in the needs of his society and religious tradition led to the conflicts that ended his life. For two-thousand years people have asked "Why did he die?", "Did he have to die?", and "What did Jesus' death accomplish?" Various Christian preachers and theologians have developed responses to these questions. These discussions often refer to the meaning of Jesus' death as "the atonement."

In a letter to Christians in the Greek city of Colossae, Saint Paul declares that "…all the fullness of God was pleased to dwell…" in Jesus Christ. (Colossians 1:19) As we have seen, Jesus' entire life tells us what God is like. Although God is a mystery beyond words, Jesus made God's presence and love tangible through his relationships with people. It is worth repeating that he fed the hungry, healed the sick, forgave sinners, and gave hope to the poor and marginalized. He proclaimed that justice and compassionate living were manifestations of God's kingdom.

Why, then, was Jesus crucified and why has the cross become a central symbol for Christians? The four gospels show clearly that Jesus did not have to die to demonstrate that God is loving, patient, and always forgiving. His intimacy with God provided a

63

way for every person to share that same relationship with God. Jesus was crucified because his passion to make God's kingdom a reality within his society conflicted with the needs of religious and political leaders who feared that Jesus' mission and popularity would weaken their control and jeopardize their attempts to maintain peaceful coexistence with Rome. Jesus was a threat to the status quo.

Jesus' death demonstrated God's unconditional love by his willingness to suffer the unjust consequences of making what God desires for human life tangible in people's lives. He was convinced that his words and actions were signs that the reign of God (kingdom of God) was being established to renew the lives of the people of Israel. "But if it is by the finger of God that I cast out the demons, then the kingdom of God has come to you." (Luke 11:20) Jesus died because he was passionate about life. This commitment to costly love and the reign of God released an energy that raised him beyond the limitations of death. The death and resurrection of Jesus transformed the lives of those who followed him. They too became passionate about life. Their experiences of the risen Christ and the communities they formed to continue Jesus' mission are recorded in the books of the New Testament.

Jesus' death on a cross is an invitation to embody that same love and share his passion to make God's kingdom a reality in our daily lives. *"And I, when I am lifted up from the earth, will draw all people to myself."* (John 12:32) The cross has become a symbol and reminder of how much we are loved and invites us to be drawn into that love and make that love tangible in the way we live. The vocation of all Christians today is to continue Jesus commitment to making the reign of God a reality in modern society.

A misunderstanding of atonement

In Christian theology and teaching, atonement often means "what Jesus has done for us." In this context "the atonement" sometimes refers to the death of Jesus as the means through which human beings gain merit in a legalistic sense to become acceptable to God.

This assumes that we have become "not acceptable" because of our sins or lack of belief and something has to happen to change God's mind about us. This theological perspective is not congruent with the Bible or with the life and teaching of Jesus. It is responsible for much unnecessary guilt and pain, gives a false and unnecessarily austere image of God, and affects the nature of prayer. What we think of God affects the way we pray and live. It will affect, also, our attitude toward death.

An elder's fear of dying

In the early 1990s I was helping lead a day retreat in Phoenix, Arizona for residents of a retirement community. In an afternoon session some of the participants wanted to discuss their fears surrounding dying. When I asked, "What do you fear the most?," a woman became agitated and replied, "I'm worried about what will happen to me when I die, because I don't believe everything in my denomination's statement of faith. My pastor says it is important to believe all of it, but I can't. I'm afraid."

This woman's fear was real and at the same time completely unnecessary. Why would her pastor challenge a person in her 70s this way? The pastor is concerned for her, yet his pressure for her to "believe" everything required by his denomination places the emphasis on the denomination's theology rather than a biblical understanding of God as patient and compassionate. In emphasizing the denomination's statement of faith the pastor seems to give more importance to theology *about* God than the woman's personal relationship *with* God and her life-long devotion to her faith community. Will a statement of faith negate God's unconditional love for this woman? Will God abandon her when she dies?

This elder's fear of dying without "right belief" is an example of the pain caused by religious teaching that is not congruent with the life and teaching of Jesus. In this incident, the fear is caused by a person's experience of pressure from a pastor's authority. That authority minimized the integrity of the elder's experience of God. Later in the day, the retreat leader and I listened to her describe her devotion to Jesus and reassured her of Jesus' unconditional love for her that will transcend death.

A biblical understanding of atonement:

In order to understand the original meaning of Jesus' death it is important to explore what sacrifice, atonement, and redemption meant in the context of first-century Judaism. Although Jesus did not seek crucifixion, he was well aware that his passion to make the reign of God tangible among his people and faith community could lead to his death. He was willing to make this sacrifice, although he earnestly hoped it would not be necessary. *"Father, if you are willing, remove this cup from me; yet, not my will, but yours be done."* (Luke 22:42) It was perfectly natural for Jesus, his disciples, and later St. Paul (a learned Pharisee and devout Jew) to interpret the events leading up to his crucifixion, his death, and his resurrection through the eyes of their Jewish understanding of the ways sin and alienation from God can be healed. Keep in mind that this process, for the Jews, was very down-to-earth and not abstract.

Sacrifice in the Hebrew tradition

In the first century, the sacrifice of an animal or fowl had the practical purpose of restoring a pure and harmonious relationship between God and an individual or the whole people of Israel. The gift of a sacrificed animal or fowl was a necessity to maintain a person's life or the life of the whole people. Their whole world became sanctified and their blessedness before God was restored. The sanctity of the offering restored the sanctity of the person who offered it. Both God and the person offering the sacrifice are honored and the covenant between them is strengthened. "In the sacrifice all the threads of life are gathered together. Renewed life springs from sacrifice, because the blessing is recreated in it, and its effects are felt in all the forces of life, in the world of God, the world of man, and the world of nature."[34]

When Jesus spoke of "sinners", and "sinners" are mentioned in the book of Acts and the letters of St. Paul, the meaning refers to persons who have either rejected or, by their behavior, have departed from fulfilling the Torah. Since the Torah is the path toward life, they have rejected the life God offers and the blessing—the life force of the soul—God desires to give each person. The Israelites believed that the life (soul) of a living being resided in the blood of that being. Therefore, the sacrificial shedding of blood releases the life-force of the animal or fowl. This offering of life has the effect of restoring the life of the person offering the sacrifice to the life of God and brings blessing to God as well. This is why both the Hebrew Scriptures and the New Testament refer to "God's wrath" as a response to rejection of God's desires. Intentional sinful acts alienate the sinner from God and repudiate the sacredness of human life. In early Israel the awareness of the "wrath of God" toward unrepentant "sinners" used a human emotion to describe God's response to sin. Yet in both the Old and New Testaments God's "anger" is coupled with God's patient desire to forgive and restore the sinner or in some cases the entire nation. Anxiety and fear of God's wrath became, in some, a motivation for sacrifice that would "turn away" God's anger and open a path for reconciliation. The prophet Ezekiel made it clear that God has *"...no pleasure in the death of anyone, says the Lord God. Turn then, and live."* (Ezekiel 18:32)

Ancient Israelite sacrifices are often misunderstood today. To some they seem crude and grotesque, to others unnecessary. Sometimes they are characterized as "buying God's favor." These reactions fail to see the indigenous motivations for these cultic practices mentioned in the previous paragraphs. Without successful crops and a healthy supply of animals, the lives of the people would be in jeopardy. The offerings of "first-fruits" of crops and the sacrifice of animals, the life of crops, animals, and human beings demonstrate complete dependence on God. As these gifts of life are returned to God, the sanctity of life is renewed and God, as original giver, is blessed. The sacrificial gift and the giver are "absorbed" into the holiness of God, the source of all holiness.[35] When an animal is sacrificed, the blood (which contains the soul of the animal and its species) burnt on the altar becomes a prayer offered to God and the "fruitfulness" of the animal is restored. The person making the offering shares in the sanctification of the offering. Then the person or family feasts on the flesh of the animal in celebration of God's gift. As we have seen, the whole process acknowledges God as the source of life and holiness and the desire of the giver for the renewal of life and holiness.

Sin in the Hebrew tradition

The Israelites were very conscious of "sin." When a human being acts in defiance of God's laws (the Torah) that person alienates him- or herself from God and other people. The sanctity of life is profaned and shame is brought upon the person and his- or her family. The offering of an animal acknowledges the holiness of what is offered and the desire of the person or group making the offering for the renewal of their relationship with God and their community. The person shares in the return of the animal to God. The sacrifice represents the person's desire for his or her restoration of holiness or "redemption."

Within this desire is the awareness that, although God has stern words for sinful behavior, behind those words is God's passionate desire that each sinner will acknowledge his or her sins and seek forgiveness. The Hebrew prophet Joel speaks clearly about God's desire for the transformation of each sinner: *"For he is gracious and full of mercy, slow to anger, and abounding in loving kindness, and relenting of evil."* (Joel 2:13) The sinner's desire for forgiveness and God's mercy and loving kindness provide a path toward redemption.

Redemption in the Hebrew tradition

The Israelites placed great emphasis on redemption. It was a powerful metaphor signifying God's desire and action to restore a person who has sinned (departed from the Torah) to that person's original relationship with God, based on the covenant. It restores their life. Redemption also refers to the restoration of property that is stolen or damaged. It amends for injury or the taking of a life. One person can redeem another person from their obligations. In the first century redemption often referred to the freeing of slaves to their former way of life. Thus, redemption refers to restoration of a person's authentic life.

In ancient Israel "atonement" also referred to "covering up" or "blotting out" the memory of sinful acts. There are many examples in the prophets and some of the psalms. God prefers mercy to wrathful judgment. *"Seek the Lord while he may be found, call upon him while he is near; let them return to the Lord, that he may have mercy on them, and to our God, for he will abundantly pardon."* (Isaiah 55:6–7) *"Have mercy on me, O God, according to your steadfast love; according to your abundant mercy blot out my transgressions."* (Psalm 51:1) *"Is Ephraim my dear son? Is he the child I delight in? As often as I speak against him, I still remember him. Therefore I am deeply moved for him; I will surely have mercy on him, says the Lord."* (Jeremiah 31:20) When Jesus was criticized by some Pharisees for being in the presence of sinners he responded, *"Go and learn what this means, 'I desire mercy, not sacrifice.' For I have come to call not the righteous but sinners."* (Matthew 9:13) Jesus is most likely referring to the words of God in the prophet Hosea, *"For I desire steadfast love and not sacrifice, the knowledge [i.e. experience] of God rather than burnt offerings."* (Hosea 6:6)

The suffering servant image

In Isaiah there is the central role of "the suffering servant" (another graphic metaphor understood both as an individual and as the nation as a whole) whose willingness to suffer restores the relationship of the people to God. *"Is it too light a thing that you should be my servant to raise up the tribes of Jacob and to restore the survivors of Israel; I will give you as a light to the nations, that my salvation may reach to the ends of the earth."* (Isaiah 49:6)

The first-century context for Jesus' death

It is easy to see how Jesus, his disciples, and the earliest Followers of the Way, including St. Paul, would try to understand the significance of Jesus's death on the cross using their own experiences and understanding of sacrifice, redemption, and atonement. It is no surprise that the New Testament used these words (in their first century context and meaning) to interpret the meaning and significance of Christ's death. *It is important to see these words in their first century context before we make conclusions about their meaning based on modern usage and theological reflection.* In a general sense, the New Testament proclamation is that Jesus' death reconciles persons to God through their union with Christ in his death. *"And I, when I am lifted up from the earth, will draw all people to myself."* (John 12:32) The action is initiated by God because of love and not wrath. The result is that by sharing in Christ's death (and therefore being drawn into his life) a person shares in his resurrected and transformed life. In this context, atonement means that God, in Christ, already loves human beings. *God's mind does not have to be changed because we have sinned.* God's desire is for us to see this love in Christ and let go of our desire to be in control of our lives. This acceptance of God's love will restore us to the authentic nature of human life that Jesus demonstrated in his life. This is what St. Paul means by living "in Christ." What Paul has in mind comes into clearer focus when we recall his understanding of the death of Christ as a lesson demonstrating how authentic humankind should live, *"...he died for all that those who live might live no longer for themselves."* (2 Corinthians 5:15)[36]

In his letter to Christians in Ephesus, Paul reminds them of the radical change Christ's death and resurrection made in their lives. *"Your world was a world without hope and without God. But now, in union with Christ Jesus, you who were once far off have been brought near through the shedding of Christ's blood. For he is himself our peace."* (Ephesians 2:12–14) Paul is using his first century Jewish understanding of sacrifice and atonement to proclaim the transformation that is made possible through Jesus' death and resurrection. **As Jesus said before he died, people will be drawn to him and in that intimate relationship will experience "shalom." They are restored to fullness of life. This is the biblical meaning of atonement.**

The Biblical understanding of atonement recognizes the reality of sin and the ways in which human beings fail to live compassionate lives according to the Torah. Atonement recognizes that the source of our compassion is the life of God. To be at one with God is to be open to the flow of divine life. The doctrine of the atonement testifies that God's love is unconditional and that God continually reaches out, in the midst of human sinfulness, to restore a relationship of oneness.

The implications of atonement for modern life

As we have seen, Jesus' death demonstrated God's unconditional love by his willingness to suffer the unjust consequences of making what God desires for human life tangible in people's lives. He died because he was passionate about life. This commitment to costly love released an energy that raised him beyond the limitations of death.

Atonement, then, is the flow of our lives into the heart of God. *"And I, when I am lifted up from the earth, will draw all people to myself."* (John 12:32) We should carry these words with us every day because it is possible for each of us to obscure or interrupt this natural flow. *Think of atonement as the daily release of everything that holds us back from being one with God.* Our truest and most authentic identity or self is found in God, who is already present in each of us. Sin is our denial and rejection of our authentic self and the fullness of our life in God. The consequences of sinful behavior block the manifestation of the image of God in each of us and bring hardship and evil into daily life. It alienates us from God and other people. The image of God in us, the sanctity and divine potential of our human life, is never erased by sin. Atonement happens often in our lives as God continually calls us back to our true identity and releases us from all that holds us back from abundant life in God.

Atonement and prayer

Prayer is the flow of the *energy of God.* It is not possible for us to understand or experience the essence of God. This does not mean that God is distant or uninvolved in our lives. The *Spirit of God* flows out from God's essence, from the divine mystery, and becomes manifest in time and space and in the heart of every human being. The flow of God's energy became manifest in a unique way in Jesus of Nazareth. In Jesus' life we witness a constant flow of his life into the heart of God and of God's love into the heart of Jesus. This flow of energy is what Jesus called the *Spirit*. It became the source of all his words and actions. It was his consciousness and the source of his power and wisdom. It was a manifestation of the *love of God.* This is what John the Evangelist means when he says that God is love. We are able to know God through the language of love. The flow of love between Jesus and God, whom he called Abba and the Holy One was the flow of the Spirit between them. This flow of God's energy is what we call *prayer.* Jesus made it very clear to those who were close to him that this prayer was the source of his life here on earth and that this same life of prayer was possible for every person who is willing to accept it. One aspect of atonement, then, is the willingness to take on, to make room for, *the consciousness of Jesus.* It is the humanness of Jesus which makes it possible for us to have the same flow of prayer between ourselves and God that he experienced. It is the *gift of the Spirit* which makes it possible. The image Jesus used for taking on the consciousness he possessed is that of "dying to self." *"Then Jesus told his disciples, 'If any want to be my followers, let them deny themselves and take up their cross and follow me. For those who want to save their life will lose it, and those who lose their life for my sake will find it. For what will it profit them if they gain the whole world but forfeit their life? Or what will they give in return for their life?'"* (MT 16:24–26) At the heart of atonement is the willingness to let go of control of ourselves in order to release the flow of Christ's consciousness in us. This is what Jesus desired for every person in his lifetime here on earth.

Atonement and the crucifixion of Jesus

Jesus did not have to die on the cross to release us from what holds us back from being one with God. His life and teaching, as well as his compassionate engagement with society, form a Way toward true and authentic living. This Way is not simply one more rational plan for effective and wholesome human life. The Way of Jesus is unique because it is not *his* way. It is the wisdom and power of God manifest through him. *"I can do nothing on my own. As I hear, I judge; and my judgment is just, because I seek to do not my own will but the will of him who sent me."* (John 5:30) *"My teaching is not mine but his who sent me."* (John 7:16) Jesus knew, while he was still alive, that it is his Abba's delight to give us the reign of God. Jesus knew that God will instill in our hearts the desire to see the world and ourselves through God's eyes and the courage to respond with compassionate living. Is this really possible? *"Do not be afraid little flock, for it is your Father's good pleasure to give you the kingdom."* (Luke 12:32)

Jesus knew that execution would be an almost certain consequence of his spiritual path and teaching. He did not accept this without a difficult interior struggle. Jesus accepted death because he would not deny his true self as God's "Son of Man" in order to appease the self-serving power of the religious and political leaders of his day. In Jesus' heritage, the Son of Man was a name and image for a person whose life would manifest the presence of God and make a spiritual transformation of society possible. Jesus' love for all those around him, including those who condemned him, was too powerful to allow false values to prevail over his personal experience of true human life. He accepted death to stand firm for authentic life. He was practicing what he preached.

After the Last Supper in Jerusalem Jesus walked with his disciples across the Kidron Valley to the Mount of Olives where he entered deeply into prayer—aware that death was near, asking if it could somehow be avoided, but trusting his Abba's will. Then he gets up and speaks to his disciples who had fallen asleep, exhorting them to pray as well about the danger that lay ahead. *"While he was still speaking, suddenly a crowd came, and the one called Judas, one of the twelve, was leading them. He approached Jesus to kiss him; but Jesus said to him, 'Judas, is it with a kiss that you are betraying the Son of Man?' When those who were around him saw what was coming, they asked, 'Lord, should we strike them with a sword?' Then one of them struck the slave of the high priest and cut off his right ear. But Jesus said, 'No more of this!' And he touched his ear and healed him."* (Luke 22:47–51) Jesus' non-violent response was a powerful statement that he knew they had no idea of the emptiness of their values and power. *"Then Jesus said to the chief priests, the officers of the temple police, and the elders who had come out for him, 'Have you come out with swords and clubs as if I were a bandit? When I was with you day after day in the temple, you did not lay hands upon me. But this is your hour, and the power of darkness!'"* (Luke 23:52–53)

Jesus, at the time of his trial and execution, was faced with the reality of physical death in order to stand firm for authentic human life. He had faced a similar trial in the wilderness following his baptism. In the desert he had let go of a personal vision of worldly security and popularity and power in order to gain a vision of God which led to fullness of life. On the cross he faced another letting go, a letting go of physical life and a letting go of any awareness that God would use conventional force to free him from his challenge. Jesus was facing the consummation of his own teaching: *"For those who want to save their life will lose it, and those who lose their life for my sake will find it."* (Matthew 16:25). Jesus' death, while not necessary (certainly not necessary to appease a "God" who was angry because of human sin), had the effect—as Jesus had sensed during his lifetime—of drawing others to let go of their false visions of human life in order to find the same life in God which Jesus experienced and knew to be true. In this way Jesus does something we cannot do for ourselves. God, present in his life draws us to fullness of life in God.

Atonement and the Resurrection of Jesus:

Jesus' willingness to die to everything that limits human life released a new dimension of life within him. The dynamic power of God raised him beyond the limitations of death.

As Jesus had done so often during his earthly lifetime, after his resurrection he invites persons who are willing to let go of self to share the new dimension of his risen life. In the words of St. Paul,

"From now on, therefore, we regard no one from a human point of view; even though we once knew Christ from a human point of view, we know him no longer in that way. So if anyone is in Christ, there is a new creation: everything old has passed away; see, everything has become new!" (2 Corinthians 5:16–17)

The effect of Jesus' death (the atonement) is not to change God's mind about us, but to change our minds about ourselves. The "newness" is the renewal of a relationship with God that has always been with us. As we have seen, according to Jesus' Jewish heritage, our original nature shares the goodness of God. We are created in the image of God and nothing can eliminate that original human sanctity. Sin is the myriad ways our behavior denies this relationship. But the reality of sin does not define who we are. It is not authentic human life. Jesus' life, death, and resurrection open our eyes so that we can embrace our original nature again. Jesus promises nothing less than we shall *"…become participants of the divine nature."* (2 Peter 1:5) In St. Paul's words, *"For we are the temple of the living God…"* (2 Corinthians 6:16b)

Atonement is not a once-for-all thing. It is a daily recognition of our original nature and that vision opens a path—empowered by the Holy Spirit—for the renewal of our relationship with God. It is a never-ending mystery.

The joy we celebrate during the Easter season is not limited to the fact that Jesus is risen. The joy flows, also, from the realization of what Jesus' resurrection makes possible in our lives. His resurrection makes our resurrection possible because we will be truly animated by the risen life of Christ Jesus and, as he promised before his death, we will be penetrated by his Spirit.

"If you love me, you will keep my commandments. And I will ask the Father, and he will give you another Advocate, to be with you forever. This is the Spirit of truth, whom the world cannot receive, because it neither sees him nor knows him. You know him [experience him] because he abides with you, and he will be in you. I will not leave you orphaned; I am coming to you. In a little while the world will no longer see me, but you will see me; because I live, you also will live. On that day you will know that I am in my Father, and you in me, and I in you. They who have my commandments and keep them are those who love me; and those who love me will be loved by my Father, and I will love them and reveal myself to them." (John 14:15–21)

Atonement is rooted in experience

The life, death, and resurrection of Jesus form a single event that exhorts us to live into the transformed and authentic human life the resurrection of Christ makes possible. This is Good News! It is not about words, abstract theology or wisdom. It is about *experiencing* abundant life in the day-to-day ordinariness of each of our lives. It is also an organic relationship.

"As you therefore have received Christ Jesus the Lord, continue to live your lives in him, rooted and built up in him and established in the faith, just as you were taught, abounding in thanksgiving." (Colossians 1:6–7)

The New Testament is a record of the myriad ways God was experienced in people's lives through their relationships with Jesus of Nazareth during his earthly life and after his resurrection. That experience transformed their lives and motivated them to share their down-to-earth experience with others.

"We declare to you what was from the beginning, and what we have heard, what we have seen with our eyes, what we have looked at and touched with our hands, concerning the word of life—this life was revealed, and we have seen it and testify to it, and declare to you

the eternal life that was with the Father and was revealed to us—we declare to you what we have seen and heard so that you also may have fellowship with us, and truly our fellowship is with the Father and with his Son Jesus Christ. We are writing these things so that our joy may be complete." (1 John 1:1–4)

Chapter 7

The Meaning and Purpose of Human Life: Jesus and the Trinity

"For the things of the Trinity are seen dimly,
and are understood only so much."
Simeon the New Theologian (949–1022)

The "Trinity" is not an intellectual definition of God. It is a symbol that discloses three ways human beings in the Judeo-Christian tradition have experienced God's love. These experiences of God's presence in creation reflect God's desire to enter into a relationship with us. They enable us to see the active diversity and energy within the single reality of God's nature. We do not determine what God is like. God takes the initiative to love us in time and space and our response completes God's invitation to participate in a communion of being. The Trinity is our limited way of describing our experience of this eternal mystery. Some early Christian teachers called this relationship "dancing with God." In the dance we discover what God is like and in the process discover the human vocation to manifest God's nature in the way we live.

Many people, including devout Christians, have a problem with the Trinity. Some think the Trinity is unnecessary. Why not just focus on Jesus? Others think the "doctrine" of the Trinity makes it difficult for Christians to be in dialog with other religious traditions. I have encountered many people who just can't wrap their heads around what appears to be an intellectual understanding of what God is like. If there is only one God, why is God divided into three "persons?" One person asked me, "If Jesus was divine, whom was he praying to when he said his prayers?"

So why is the Trinity an essential part of Christian experience of God? What would the Christian path be like without the Trinity? Are we just hanging on to an outdated piece of theology?

At the heart of difficulties understanding the Trinity is human language and human social communities. Our language about God is most often related to human experience and relationships. The Bible is full of descriptions of God and God's activities using language about ourselves, our emotions and our culture. We have to use language that is related to our experience. And when we encounter things that go beyond human experience and understanding, poetry, myth, metaphor, and other artistic mediums help us describe and embrace what conventional, intellectual language is unable to express. Karl Rahner, a deeply prayerful Roman Catholic theologian has expressed his own frustration with the limitations of words and knowledge.

"And no matter how faithful I may be to [knowledge], it can never really cure me. All it can give me is words and concepts, which perform the middle-man's service of expressing and interpreting reality to me, but it can never still my heart's craving for the reality, itself, for true life and true possession. I shall never be cured until all reality comes streaming like an ecstatic, intoxicating melody in my heart."[37]

The verbal image of God as Father, Son, and Holy Spirit is a sacramental description that expresses the nature of God—a divine mystery—within the limitations of human language. As we have seen, it is not meant to be an intellectual "definition" of God. It is more poetic than clinical. It is an outward expression of an inner spiritual reality. It is not literal, but it is true. It expresses what is real based on human experience and declares that within God's mystical nature is a dynamic relationship revealed in a variety of human experiences of God as creator, in human encounters of the fullness of God's presence in the life of Jesus of Nazareth, and in the invisible flow of God's energies—the Spirit—within human lives and throughout the cosmos. **These three aspects of God's nature express both unity and diversity. From our point of view they are different, yet they are not separate. The fullness of God is present in each of the three manifestations of God's nature.**

Despite the limitations of its language, the image of the Trinity bears essential truths about the Christian path and human life. As St. Paul says, "We see through a glass darkly…", yet what we see tells us that the universe, our solar system and human life are not random physical and biological accidents. They are manifestations of divine love. We glimpse the sacredness of life and through the fullness of God present in Jesus' life we learn that the authentic nature and responsibilities of human life are to make divine love tangible. And lest we think that we are in control, the image of the Trinity reminds us that it is the energy of the Holy Spirit that makes all this possible.

The way of communion

Using another image from human experience, the three manifestations of God's nature may be seen as a divine *community* energized by mutual love. This divine community is the source of authentic human community. We learn how to live with each other by experiencing the relationship that exists between the three ways God cares for us. The experiences of God as creator, in the life of Jesus, and in the energies of the Spirit demonstrate a relationship within God's nature that reveals what God desires for human relationships.

Another consequence of human experience of God as Trinity is what Christians call "the incarnation." We learn from the four gospels and the remainder of the New Testament that God, the creator, entered and experienced human life in the life of Jesus of Nazareth. St Paul describes the incarnation in this way: "He is the image of the invisible God…For in him all the fullness of God was pleased to dwell…" (Colossians 1:15; 19)

All this may sound fine. But you don't have to take my personal word for it. I am part of a larger community of persons who have experienced these truths throughout thousands of years of its life. How do we know that God is "real?" How do we discover the meaning and purpose of human life? And what will make that kind of life possible? Where do we look?

As Christians, we find a three-fold context for all this in the Bible. It is the story of God's encounters with human beings, our responses to these experiences and the relationships and communities created through God's presence in human lives. This context is not assent to intellectual or dogmatic formulations. It is an understanding of the reality of God based on human experience. As we experience God's presence we will discover what it means to be human. Without this experience, the words of the Bible would just be words.

The Bible demonstrates a three-fold context for discovering the meaning and purpose of authentic human life.

God the Creator

"In the beginning God created the heavens and the earth..."

Our feeble attempts to define the ineffable are eclipsed by the wonder of God's presence in creation.

"The heavens are telling the glory [presence] of God; and the firmament proclaims his handiwork. Day to day pours forth speech, and night to night declares knowledge. There is no speech, nor are there words; there voice is not heard; yet their voice goes out through all the earth, and their words to the end of the world." (Psalm 19:1-4)

Human beings are born with a sense of wonder, that graceful openness to be acted upon by the mystery and vitality at the heart of life. Within us and all around us are opportunities to become aware of another natural dimension of life. Far too often our vision is blurred by our busyness and preoccupation with controlling every aspect of life. Our modern culture conditions us not to trust those vulnerable moments when ordinary things and persons enable us to experience a divine or transcendent presence.

Wonder is a gateway to the spiritual dimension of life. It is not a sector of life. The Judeo-Christian tradition proclaims that human beings have been created with a spiritual dimension that permeates every aspect of our lives. Human life in the world around us, with its obvious limitations, is the venue for experiencing God's presence and being transformed (completed) by that Presence. The biblical narrative declares that we are created in the image of God and that our vocation as human beings is to manifest God's likeness and nature in the way we live.

Spiritual formation is the variety of ways we discover God's presence in creation and our myriad personal responses to that Presence. The biblical story of God's encounters with human beings almost always begins with our awareness of God as creator of heaven and earth.

God the Son

> The incarnation of God in Jesus of Nazareth:
> St. Paul declares, *"For in him all the fullness of God*
> *was pleased to dwell…"*
> *(Colossians 1:19)*

The incarnation of God in Jesus demonstrates what union with God in a human life is like. At the same time, the presence of the fullness of God in Jesus makes it possible for every human being to share that same relationship.

Jesus' passionate desire was transmission of experience of God.

> "The Father and I are one…
> the Father is in me and I am in the Father."
> *(John 10:30&38)*

> *"I have made your name known to those whom you gave me…I*
> *ask not only on behalf of these, but also on behalf of those who*
> *will believe in me through their word, that they may all be one.*
> *As you, Father, are in me and I am in you, may they also be in*
> *us, so that the world may know you have sent me."*
> *(John 17:6&20-21)*

This sacred promise is described in the second letter of Peter:

"By his divine power, he has given us all things that we need for life and for true devotion, bringing us to know God himself, who has called us to his own glory and goodness. In making these gifts, he has given us the guarantee of something very great and wonderful to come: through them you will be able to share the divine nature and to escape corruption in a world that is sunk in vice."

(2 Peter 1:3-4 Jerusalem Bible translation)

Sharing God's divine nature means making God's attributes and goodness tangible in our daily life. The life of Jesus shows us what that looks like. That is why Jesus exhorted people to "follow me." St. Paul uses a vivid poetic image to describe what happens when a person becomes a disciple of Jesus:

"I have been crucified with Christ; and it is no longer I who live, but it is Christ who lives in me." (Galatians 2:20)

The intimacy with God that Jesus desires for us provides the context for authentic human life. Our life with God reveals the sacred nature of human life and the world around us. When human life is lived out of context it is in danger of losing its true meaning and purpose. The result can be alienation from God, ourselves, our neighbor, and the world.

We become fully human only insofar as we experience God and share in God's nature. How is this kind of life possible?

God the Holy Spirit

"What [person] *can know the intentions of God?*
Who can divine the will of God?"[38]
"…the depths of God can only be known
by the Spirit of God."[39]

The gift of the Holy Spirit

During his lifetime Jesus of Nazareth was a visible example of what it means to participate in the nature of God, both in his actions and teaching. He proclaimed that his words and actions not only came from his "Father", but will lead persons to the Father. It is worth repeating that as awareness of his death approached he reassured his disciples that their lives as disciples would continue; he would not leave them alone.

> *"If you love me, you will keep my commandments. And I will ask the Father, and he will give you another Advocate, to be with you forever. This is the Spirit of truth, whom the world cannot receive, because it neither sees him nor knows him. You know him, because he abides with you, and he will be in you. I will not leave you orphaned; I am coming to you. In a little while the world will no longer see me, but you will see me; because I live, you also will live. On that day you will know that I am in the Father, and you in me, and I in you.* (John 14:15-20)

> *"Nevertheless I tell you the truth: it is to your advantage that I go away, for if I do not go away, the Advocate will not come to you; but if I go, I will send him to you…I still have many things to say to you, but you cannot bear them now. When the Spirit of truth comes, he will guide you all into the truth; for he will not speak to you on his own, but will speak whatever he hears, and he will declare to you the things that are to come."* (John 16:7 & 12-13)

The Spirit is God's way of remaining close to us. The Spirit takes the initiative by opening space within us to receive and respond to God's love. At the same time the Spirit's presence in us completes our creation. The Hebrew book of Genesis describes the creation of human beings in this way: *"…then the Lord God formed man from the dust of the ground, and breathed into his nostrils the breath of life; and the man became a living being."* (Genesis 2:7)

Jesus, in a conversation with the Jewish teacher Nicodemus, declared that *"Very truly I tell you, no one can enter the kingdom of God without being born of water and Spirit. What is born of the flesh is flesh, and what is born of the Spirit is spirit."* (John 3:5-6)

Later, after Jesus' resurrection, *"Jesus came and stood among* [the disciples] *and said, 'Peace be with you.'…When he had said this, he breathed on them and said to them, 'Receive the Holy Spirit."* (John 20:19 & 22)

The breath of Jesus transmits the Spirit within his life to the lives of the disciples. In the same way that God's breath made Adam a living creature, Jesus completes the creation of the disciples' lives. Before his death Jesus said, *"I came that they may have life, and have it abundantly."* (John 10:10) Every person seeks abundant life and this yearning for meaning and purpose is the movement of the breath of the Spirit within us. The Spirit calls each person to discover and desire her or his authentic self. In John's gospel Jesus called this a "second birth" that completes and transforms each human life. *"What is born of the flesh is flesh, and what is born of the Spirit is spirit. Do not be astonished that I said to you, 'You must be born from above.'"* We are not complete until we are born of both flesh and spirit. (John 3:1–8)

This means that the Holy Spirit will wrap us in an environment of grace that transcends our limited awareness and experiences of life. Just when we reach the limitations of our personal power to meet the challenges of daily living or get lost in a vortex of digital activity searching for relationships and a reason for being alive, the Spirit will remind us that we have not reached the limits of what is possible. Sometimes when things seem empty and life is dragging, the Spirit is at work in us, silently. *"When the Spirit of truth comes, he will guide you all into the truth; for he will not speak to you on his own, but will speak whatever he hears, and he will declare to you the things that are to come."* (John 16:13) It is not easy to trust that fullness is present within the emptiness. It takes courage to have patience and continue the work of our daily lives. As we shall see in chapter 8, this is where *experience* of the Spirit in silent prayer and involvement in a local Christian community will expand the boundaries of what we think is possible.

The reality of God's triune nature: A Summary

In the Christian tradition, the context for the meaning and purpose of human life is this three-fold experience of God. Although the essence God is a mystery, our awareness of what God is like is revealed in three ways human beings have encountered God. We have learned what God is like from our experiences of God as Creator, God incarnate in Jesus of Nazareth, and the Holy Spirit. Almost all our attempts to describe the ways we apprehend God are reflections on these experiences of God and, by necessity, use terms based on human experience. Mystical or contemplative experiences of God without images or intellectual descriptions are also part of human experience of God. These experiences are recorded in the Hebrew and Christian scriptures. The Bible is a record of over 2,000 years of experiences of God and the ways Jews and Christians have responded to these experiences. Christians have added another 1,900 years of experiences. Since God is a mystery, we have used a variety of literary forms to describe these encounters and what we have learned from them. Life experience, words, quiet listening, and attention to the Spirit of truth are the most common ways we learn about what God is like. The desert father Isaac the Syrian said, "Love silence above all things, because it brings you close to fruit that the tongue cannot express." **If we seek the fruits of the Spirit, we must spend time with God.**

Biblical narratives and images reveal three ways we have encountered God:

- God is creator and sustainer of life (the mystery Jesus called "Father")

- God is encountered in the human life, death, and resurrection of Jesus (who is called "Son")

- God continues to create and sustain life through the presence and energies of God's Spirit (the Holy Spirit)

In worship Christians respond, in thanksgiving, to our triune experience of God using the familiar hymn: *Glory to the Father, and to the Son, and to the Holy Spirit; as it was in the beginning, is now, and will be forever.* This hymn reflects both the timeless mystery of God and the three ways we have experienced God in the context of our daily lives.

The reality of diversity within unity: the way of communion

Our three-fold experiences of God show us what God is like but do not infer that God is three separate persons (in a human sense of individual persons.) We have experienced the mystical reality of God in three diverse ways, yet these attributes of God's being are united in a relationship of full communion and mutual love. Although we may experience each of these aspects of God's being as unique, all aspects of God's being are present in each other. God is a communion of being. This is what John the Evangelist realized when he wrote, "In the beginning was the Word, and the Word was with God, and the Word was God." (John 1:1) When we look at an image of Jesus on the cross we are looking at the fullness of God. This communion within the essence of God is the source of all human community. It declares the sacredness and inter-dependence of all human life. The unity and diversity in God's being reveal God's desires for human society. We are called to desire and manifest an environment of communion in all our relationships. This is far from easy. Once again, Jesus is our mentor.

How do we experience and share God's presence in our daily lives?

The life of Jesus of Nazareth enables us to know what God is like and at the same time offers a path to experiencing divine life. He said, *"I am the way, the truth and the life."* Jesus exhorts us to follow him and he shows us the way. The four New Testament canonical gospels describe a four-fold pattern in Jesus' life that was at the heart of his experience of God:

- quiet listening in prayer
- faithful discernment of God's desires for his life and the world
- commitment to the scriptures and life of his Jewish religious community

- compassionate engagement in the lives of people around him

Over the past 1,900 years a variety of Christian communities have been called and guided by the Holy Spirit to experience and transmit experience of God in a similar pattern:

- a discipline of meditation and personal prayer (being with and listening to the One we desire and who desires our presence)
- a discipline of study and meditation on the Bible (not just for information, but listening to the Spirit and discernment of God's desires)
- active personal engagement in the needs of the world, guided by discernment in prayer
- commitment to the life of a faith community, especially participation in the presence of the risen Christ in the Eucharist (Holy Communion)

Discipleship requires discipline

As we have seen, the Second Letter of Peter proclaims the good news that in Christ we are called to participate in the nature of God. It is possible for our lives to make attributes of God's nature tangible in the way we live. The same passage in Second Peter goes on to declare that this will require earnest discipline as we collaborate with God.

> "For this very reason, you must make every effort to support your faith with goodness, and goodness with knowledge, and knowledge with self-control, and self-control with endurance, and endurance with godliness, and godliness with mutual affection, and mutual affection with love. For if these things are yours and are increasing among you, they will keep you from being ineffective and unfruitful in the knowledge [experience] of our Lord Jesus Christ." (2 Peter 1:5-7)

Living as a disciple of Jesus requires disciplined stewardship of our life with God. The next chapter will focus on ways Jesus is present in our lives today and make suggestions for following him.

Chapter 8

Where Is Jesus Now?

"…hearing all that Jesus was doing,
they came to him in great numbers."
Mark 3:8

People came to Jesus in great numbers while he was alive. Where is Jesus today? How will we find him? What will we experience? What difference will it make in our lives? Why bother?

Jesus anticipated questions like these when he realized that his ministry and teaching might result in his death. He made bold statements to encourage his disciples:

"Very truly, I tell you, the one who believes in me will also do the works that I do and, in fact, will do greater works than these, because I am going to the Father." (John 14:12)

Early in his ministry Jesus discerned that his work to make the reign of God tangible in people's lives could not be limited to his personal activities. He chose disciples to join his mission. Later—just before his crucifixion—he assures his followers that they will be able to continue and expand his work.

"I have said these things to you while I am still with you. But the Advocate, the Holy Spirit, whom the Father will send in my name, will teach you everything, and remind you of all I have said to you." (John 14:25–26)

Jesus was clear that the wisdom and presence of the Spirit of God who filled and empowered his life will be present to his disciples as well. Like Jesus, their words and actions would have their origin in God. *The same is true for Jesus' followers today.*

How is this possible? Is it just "pie in the sky?" I'm reminded of one of Cassius Clay's remarks before a boxing match: "Don't give me no pie in the sky after I die. I want somethin' here on the ground while I'm still around."

Jesus offers a simple method for making a connection with him today that's here on the ground:

> *"Abide in me as I abide in you. Just as the branch cannot bear fruit by itself, unless it abides in the vine, neither can you unless you abide in me. Those who abide in me and I in them bear much fruit, because apart from me you can do nothing."* (John 15:4–5)

Perhaps the desert father Abba Paul the Simple may have had these words in mind when he said, "Stay close to Jesus." How does this happen today?

How do we experience God's presence in Jesus' life today and follow where he leads?

Once again, Jesus is our mentor. Jesus' life itself shows us the path. We can learn from the patterns in his life that guided and empowered his life and ministry. We can benefit from his experience if we desire his presence in our lives today. These prayer-filled disciplines mirror his life and will help us recognize Jesus' presence today and empower us to follow him.

- quiet listening
- faithful discernment
- commitment to the scriptures and life of a Christian faith community that includes the Jewish scriptures of the Old Testament
- compassionate engagement in the life of the world

These four patterns gave meaning, purpose, and vision to Jesus' life and to the disciples who followed him in the first century. They provide steps along a path for encountering and following Jesus today.

Quiet listening

Abba Paul the Simple reminds us of the first step: "Keep close to Jesus." ***Stay with a pattern of daily prayer.*** Remain in the company of God in the midst of unbelievably busy days. As you learn to listen to God's silent voice regularly you will learn to recognize God's voice everywhere and trust what you are hearing. St. Benedict calls this "listening with the ear of your heart." It is paying attention to God's presence in the depths of our being—a placeless place where our inner spirit and God's Spirit dwell in communion. It is an auditorium for listening to God's voice. Suggestions for daily personal prayer and meditation are given in Chapter 9.

Prayer is more than words. It is the demeanor of a humble and flexible heart that makes space in our lives for God and other people. This is why we sometimes kneel to pray. We know that we are not the center of the universe. Etty Hillesum, a Jewish writer who perished in the Holocaust, expresses an unsolicited impulse to kneel.

"A desire to kneel down sometimes pulses through my body, or rather it is as if my body has been meant and made for the act of kneeling. Sometimes, in moments of deep gratitude, kneeling down becomes an overwhelming urge, head deeply bowed, hands before my face."[40]

Whether you kneel or not, if you are bowing in spirit you will begin to see the inner reality and sanctity of people and things. We can pray for each other, along with Saint Paul:

"*I pray that you may have the power to comprehend, with all the saints, what is the breadth and length and height and depth, and to know the love of Christ that surpasses knowledge, so that you may be filled with all the fullness of God.*" (Ephesians 14-19)

The consequence of prayer is that in submitting yourself, voluntarily, to God you are changed. It is no longer you who live, but Christ who lives in you. You become real. You become the beloved person you were created to be. Love is the meaning.

Faithful discernment[41]

Our time in quiet listening and prayer will become a source of intimacy with God but its purpose is not self-centeredness. Prayer will help you see yourself, God, and the world more honestly. It will help you be *real* by showing your natural goodness and at the same time help you discern ways God is calling you to change and mature. Prayer will change your consciousness so that you will see into the deeper meaning of what is going on in your life and the world around you. It will bring you joy at the wonder of creation and the amazing creativity and variety of human beings. Prayer will also bring you sadness and righteous anger at the presence of injustice, hunger, and unnecessary conflict and abuse of other human beings. Your time apart with God will reveal ways you can speak out in response and become involved in the needs of others. Prayer will also let us know when we have become a source of pain or injustice for other persons. Prayer is not self-centered "navel-gazing" that separates you from life. It will drive you to become more fully engaged with life in the same way that the Spirit of God drove Jesus into the wilderness to pray and then out into the lives of people around him. This is the challenge of love. Opening ourselves to prayer in this way is risky. Perhaps that is why many people avoid prayer. We are reluctant to let go of control of our lives.

Commitment to the scriptures and life of a Christian faith community that include the Jewish scriptures of the Old Testament

Jesus' teaching and activities were guided and sustained by his formation in his Jewish holy scriptures and participation in the teaching and worship of his Jewish faith community.

It is tempting in our culture—and in the midst of ways in which individual Christians and churches have failed to rely on Jesus and have caused great harm in the name of Christ—to rely on ourselves and create our own spiritual path (or to reject any path!) This may be necessary for a while, but there is a danger in detaching ourselves from the life of a spiritual community. When that happens we limit our lives to what we desire and can make possible. We narrow our vision. Although forgiveness and healing may be necessary, reconciliation with faith communities that have harmed us is possible and the treasures and common life within them will provide discernment and growth, guided by the Holy Spirit. Sometimes the need for reconciliation will bring forth new and innovative ways of living as a community. This requires honest self-knowledge and the courage to risk change for the common good.

We can learn from Jesus' example.

Not long before Jesus' death and resurrection he assured his disciples, *"Wherever two or three of you are gathered in my name, I am with you."* In his culture the "name" of a person was not simply identification; it signified the person's presence and agency. Soon after Jesus' resurrection the New Testament book of Acts describes the disciples gathering in Jesus' name. *"They devoted themselves to the apostles teaching and fellowship, to the breaking of bread and the prayers...Day by day they spent much time together in the temple, they broke bread at home and ate their food with glad and generous hearts, praising God and having the goodwill of all the people. And day by day the Lord added to their number those who were being saved."* (Acts 2:42; 46–47)

Why is participating in the life of a faith community and its tradition important?

Quiet listening, faithful discernment, and personal liturgies are essential. There is no substitute for direct experience of God. At the same time, Jesus' life demonstrates an integration of personal prayer with active participation in his Jewish faith community. As we have seen, Jesus always found time to listen to God, the world around him, and his inner self. This listening heart was the source of the guidance and desire which, along with direct experience of God's love, led and sometimes drove him into compassionate involvement in the lives of others. But all this took place in the context of his active involvement in the life of his religious community. The four gospels tell us that Jesus worshipped regularly in synagogues on the Sabbath and on occasion read from and commented on the Hebrew Scriptures. He participated in the major festivals and liturgies in the Temple in Jerusalem: *Sukkot*, the Feast of Booths and the Feast of Passover, *Pesah*, and Unleavened Bread. We have seen that in the desert following his baptism Jesus responded to temptations with discernment based on his knowledge of Hebrew Scriptures. The gospels narrate Jesus' fluency in the Scriptures in the contexts of his teaching and ministry, especially the psalms and the prophets. He was not "proof texting." He experienced God's presence and guidance as he reflected on the Jewish scriptures. They formed an environment to discern God's presence and desires in his life and society.

Roots, common worship, spiritual formation, teaching, fellowship and mutual support

The roots of Jesus' Jewish faith community continued after his death and resurrection in the lives of his followers and formed a foundation for the evolution of Christian faith communities. These are timeless roots that transcend, yet are interpreted within, a variety of cultures and have sustained and empowered followers of Jesus in a variety of Christian traditions for two thousand years. A place to look for Jesus today is in the lives of persons who have entrusted their lives to the risen Christ and are committed to following him within a faith community.

A primary advantage of participation in a faith community is that it provides worship, sacraments, spiritual formation and teaching, fellowship, and opportunities for mutual support that we would miss if we design our own spiritual path. If we design our own spiritual path then we are limited to what we desire and miss opportunities to be formed by others and contribute to their spiritual lives. We limit our experience of God if we rely on ourselves.

There are many faith communities that reflect the richness of the Christian tradition. If you are not part of a faith community I recommend that you consider joining a congregation that follows the Christian liturgical year, has a focus on the sacraments—especially the Eucharist (Holy Communion), offers a variety of opportunities for spiritual formation, emphasizes study of the life of Jesus, mentors members in prayer and meditation, and involves both clergy and lay persons in the leadership of the congregation. *All these aspects form an environment of grace that will guide and empower you as a follower of Jesus.*

- The liturgical year provides a cycle of seasons, feasts, and biblical reading that covers an overview of the life of Jesus and a wide variety of biblical readings from the Hebrew Scriptures and the New Testament. A common lectionary provides a three-year cycle of readings from the four gospels and a two-year cycle of daily readings from the Bible. (For access to an ecumenical common lectionary, see the Resources section.) These cycles provide a more complete narrative of Jesus' life and our biblical heritage and inhibit preaching and teaching that may overemphasize individual parts.

- Following Jesus involves mystery. Sacraments are tangible liturgies that unite participants with an unseen mystical presence of God's Spirit. The energy of God's Spirit acts upon participants whose lives are penetrated and changed within by encounters with ordinary things like water, oil, bread, wine, hands, and touch. Sacraments are pure gifts from God. Human openness and activity is involved, but what happens is beyond our control.

- In denominations that emphasize liturgies, the Eucharist is a primary sacrament that unites participants with the presence of Jesus. In baptism the Holy Spirit fills a person's life with God's energy and that same Spirit gathers followers of Jesus to form faith communities. In this way a congregation becomes the presence of the risen Jesus in today's world. The Eucharist—from a Greek word meaning giving thanks—is usually celebrated each Sunday. Within the Eucharistic liturgy the mystical presence of Jesus is experienced in the presence of other followers of Jesus, in hearing and reflecting on portions of the Bible, and in consuming the bread and wine. Through the power of the Holy Spirit participants are filled again with Jesus' presence and are empowered to become the presence of Jesus in their daily lives.

Liturgical worship is filled with scripture, symbols, actions, mystery, and the presence of the risen Christ. It is an opportunity to temporarily leave *ordinary time* and enter *sacred time*. Although God is present in our ordinary and mundane days, sacred time gives us a different vision and experience of life. Sacred time and sacred presence, within the liturgy, will root us in life that is not tied to the limitations of chaos and human perspectives and power. Sacred time will help us see "the big picture" in the midst of instability, scatteredness, and powerlessness. The wisdom of the Bible in liturgy will help us take a longer view than what is available in ordinary time. In the Eucharistic liturgy we are reminded of who we are and once again experience Christ in ourselves, others who are present, sacred scripture, and in the sacrament of bread and wine. These are realities that chaos cannot touch or change!!

Suggestions for study and meditation on scripture are in Chapter 9.

Compassionate engagement in the life of the world

There is no common formula for following Jesus. God does not have some cosmic plan to impose on us. Each person has the opportunity to collaborate with the Holy Spirit to discern how to respond to Jesus' call, "…for it is God who is at work in you, enabling you both to will and work for his good pleasure." (St. Paul in Philippians 2:13)

In down-to-earth terms, what does it mean to "follow Jesus"? What did it mean to his disciples? Where does it lead?

In first-century Jewish culture the disciples of a rabbi learned from him by entering into his life. During Jesus' lifetime there were hundreds, perhaps well over a thousand, local teachers with disciples. They were well educated in the Hebrew Scriptures and the written and oral Torah. They were held in high esteem and were called "master", "teacher", and sometimes "rabbi." They were not simply "teachers of wisdom," conveying knowledge or advice; their goal was transformation of lives through experience. The purpose of becoming a "follower" was to learn a specific way of life; the teaching was not limited to "knowledge" or "wisdom"; the teaching was primarily being close to and sharing the life of the master/sage; teaching was by example and learning was through experience. This was the pattern of Jesus' teaching and activity. He did not have a "headquarters" or establish "wisdom schools."

Jesus made it clear in several parables that the manifestation of the reign of God in a person's life and in society is a mystery. It is like yeast in bread dough. It is like one seed of wheat that somehow can produce a hundred stalks. It is like a tiny mustard seed that will grow into a large shrub. Perhaps Saint Paul had Jesus' parable of the mustard seed in mind when he uses the image of a field to describe our life with God. "For we are God's servants, working together; you are God's field, God's building." (1 Corinthians 3:9) Jesus said:

> *"The kingdom of heaven [the reign of God] is like a mustard seed that someone took and sowed in his field; it is the smallest of all the seeds, but when it has grown it is the greatest of shrubs and becomes a tree, so that the birds of the air come and make nests in its branches."* (Matthew 13:31-32)

God has sown a tiny seed within each of us and the mysterious power of God's Spirit will make it grow and mature. You may wonder whether or not you can make a difference in the world. "What is the seed growing within me compared to the needs of the reign of God?" is a normal question. Yet what may seem small in human terms has the potential to become "*the greatest of shrubs.*" Your life can produce a tree in which other people will come and "*make nests in its branches.*" Nests are the environments for new life. Your life may seem small, but you and I are the fertile ground for the realm of God's life in the world. This aspect of following Jesus can give meaning and purpose to our lives.

Can this really happen? What are you thinking?

God's desire for human life

After Jesus' resurrection he appeared to many of the disciples in Jerusalem and Galilee. In both Luke and John's gospels, Jesus appears to disciples in a locked room in Jerusalem. Knowing they are anxious and afraid, Jesus responds to their fear saying, "*Peace be with you. As the Father has sent me, so I send you.*" Then he breathed on them and said, "*Receive the Holy Spirit…*" (John 20:21–22)

In Jesus' Hebrew culture breath conveys the vital power and life of the giver. *Jesus is transmitting his soul and energy to the disciples.* After Jesus ascension his disciples became known as the *Followers of the Way.* They remembered that Jesus had told them, "*I am the way, the truth and the life.*" (John 14:6). As we have seen, the author of the second Letter of Peter makes an audacious statement about the fundamental vocation of a follower of the risen Christ:

> "*His divine power has given us everything needed for life and godliness, through the knowledge of him who called us by his divine glory* [presence] *and goodness. Thus he has given us, through these things, his precious and very great promises, so that through them you may escape from the corruption that is in the world* [things that are futile and passing away] *because of lust* [our unrestrained ego], *and may become participants of the divine nature.*" (2 Peter 1:3–4)

The author of this letter makes it clear that Followers of the Way will participate in the same divine nature that was present in Jesus' life and led the disciples to follow him during his lifetime.

Our human lives, also, can be transformed by the divine presence. We will remain human beings, yet—as St. Paul writes—we become temples of the Holy Spirit and will manifest the risen Christ in the way we live. In Christian theology this process is called "**theosis**."

What on earth is theosis? Do we need another fancy word?

Theosis is a Greek word that means "being filled with the nature of God." Most Christians have never heard of theosis but that does not mean it is unimportant. **Theosis is another way of describing Christness.** The New Testament and early eastern Mediterranean Christian communities of faith viewed the human journey as a movement from bearing the "image" of God in our nature to becoming the "likeness" of God through our manner of life. Early theologians like Basil of Caesarea, Gregory of Nyssa and Maximos the Confessor, through earnest prayer and study of scripture, declared to their Greco-Roman culture that the human vocation is to mature from "image" to "likeness". *We are called to participate in and embody the divine nature.* This Christian perspective rejected a common dualistic philosophy of the day, which saw the human and divine natures as separate. It proclaimed that human beings are sacred and, while we are not God, we bear the "real presence" of God in time and space. We share God's nature, while remaining God's creatures.

Why is it important to make Jesus' life tangible today?

This question is "the bottom line." Does Jesus really matter today? Why bother? Jesus proclaimed constantly that without the life of God in us we will not be fully alive. Humanity will abandon its sanctity and vitality. This lack of authenticity can snuff out our life. We will lose our way. As we have seen earlier in this book, the mission of Jesus was and remains to re-orient our lives to the love and power of God so that we may be restored to fullness of human life. That is why he said, "I am the way, the truth and the life."

What does authentic human life look like?

Out of the mouths of children

In the mid-1970s my youngest son was in kindergarten and his two older brothers in early elementary school. One day I entered their room and found a hand-written sign on a wall. It was an announcement for "The Kindness Christian Club" and its rules of behavior were:

- share
- do not swear
- do not fight
- do not call names
- do not holler or shout
- do not throw trash around
- do not blow our candle out during meetings
- do not make crazy noise
- no grabbing from other kids
- be polite

Simple? Yes. Naïve? Think of the consequences of applying these "rules" to political discourse and legislation, dialogue in a polarized society, inter-personal and international relations and religious teaching and behavior. Although these "rules" were for a "Kindness Christian Club" they represent some fundamental values for authentic human life shared by all religious traditions. Substitute "compassion" for "kindness" and "community" for "club" and the wisdom of these young people mirrors some essential dimensions of what God desires in our lives.

Why bother?

Modern society is full of temptations and opportunities that masquerade as happy and satisfying life. In the end they are a detour from what is real and what we truly need. But these voices, using media and devices, proclaim their advantages constantly and at full volume everywhere we turn. Jesus, in his life of prayer, gives an example of how to listen to another voice. His quiet times guided both his teaching and his active engagement with the needs of society. He lived a contemplative life and invites us to a disciplined pattern of listening to God. As we have seen, when we listen to God through some form of meditation we will be able to hear that same voice wherever we go. And it's not a loud or coercive voice, even when it challenges us. Jesus demonstrated that the life of God is always within us, waiting for us. Jesus gives examples of what it is like to spend time in God's presence. If you want to understand what God thinks and desires for human life look at what Jesus thought and desired. Look at his life in the four gospels.

Jesus could not be clearer. His passion was for his disciples to continue his presence and mission in the world. Jesus shared God's *presence* with them—in addition to words about God's desires for the world. He declared that his intimacy with God—the womb of Jesus' compassionate engagement with society—will continue through their intimacy with him. The grace-filled energy of God's Spirit will make all this possible today.

What are you thinking?

Chapter 9 will present suggestions for personal prayer, study and meditation on the Bible, spiritual growth, and following Jesus today.

Chapter 9
———————

Staying Close to Jesus

"In a little while the world will no longer see me,
but you will see me;
because I live, you will live also.
On that day you will know that I am
in my Father, and you in me, and I in you."
John 14:19-20

"Keep close to Jesus."
The desert father Paul the Simple

In Chapter 8 we examined four patterns in Jesus' life that provide a model for us as we discover and encounter Jesus' presence in our lives today: quiet listening, faithful discernment, commitment to the scriptures and life of his Jewish religious community, and compassionate engagement with the life of the world. Here are similar patterns you and I can use to remain close to Jesus in our daily lives.

Quiet listening

What does quiet listening look like? *"In the morning, while it was still very dark, he got up and went out to a deserted place, and there he prayed."* (Mark 1:35) This was a constant pattern in Jesus' life and there is little doubt that he was influenced by his own Jewish tradition:

"O God, you are my God; at dawn I seek you; for you my soul is thirsting. For you my flesh is pining, like a weary land without water. I have come before you in the holy place, to behold your strength and your glory" (Psalm 63:2–3 Grail translation)

In our fast-paced culture it is not always convenient to make time for prayer at the beginning and end of each day. The world will come rushing in soon enough, especially if we turn on the TV or our smart phones right away. Your "holy place" is anywhere you choose to experience God's presence.

The beginning of each day

Where is your holy place at the beginning of the day? How much time can you spend there? It is important to begin simply. Soon after waking and rising, let your body express a physical sense of gratefulness for the new day and your desire to be in God's presence. Even if you know a specific day will be difficult, gratefulness and a prayer for God's love and guidance will influence your relationships and tasks.

Quiet listening first thing in the morning can be a simple prayer, sitting in silence, or reflecting on a passage of scripture from the Bible or another religious tradition. Perhaps you already have a pattern for prayer in the morning from a prayer book or your own composition.

If this is something new for you, try this at the beginning of your day:

- Get out of bed and stretch, thanking God for the new day and the gift of life: "This is the day God has given me; I will rejoice and be glad in it."

- In your "holy place" recite this prayer of verses from Psalm 63: O God, you are my God; at dawn I seek you; for you my soul is thirsting. For you my flesh is pining, like a dry, weary land without water. I have come before you in the holy place, to behold your strength and your glory.

- Your faithful love is better than life; my lips will speak your praise. I will bless you all my life; in your name I will lift up my hands. My soul shall be filled as with a banquet; with joyful lips, my mouth shall praise you.

End with one of these short prayers:

Bind my head and my heart in you, Holy One,
and may I remain in your company this day.
Bless the Lord, my soul
and bless God's holy Name.
Bless the Lord, my soul,
who leads me into love.
Into your hands I commend my spirit.

The grace of Jesus Christ, the love of God, and the companion-ship of the Holy Spirit be with me each moment of this day.

At the end of each day:

Toward the end of your day, in the evening or at bedtime, recite this prayer from the Celtic Christian tradition:

I offer to You, O God, the troubles of this day;
I lay down my burdens at your feet.
Forgive my sins;
Give me your peace, which I need not understand;
And help me receive your Word.
Into your hands I commend my family, my neighbors,
My brothers and sisters in Christ,
And every person I have met today.
The guarding of the God of life be on me,
The guarding of loving Christ be on me,
The guarding of sheltering Spirit be on me,
Every night of my life,
To aid and enfold me
Each day and night of my life.

Quiet listening does not always mean contemplative prayer in total silence and may take place at different times throughout your day. Eventually you will find it a natural and vital part of each day, regardless of the time. But whatever you decide, be sure to make it *a consistent pattern and discipline each day*. This will not be easy because our smart phones, email, Twitter, and Facebook keep us constantly accessible. There is nothing wrong with communication, conversation and entertainment. At the same time, it is possible to fill our lives with so many things that we empty life of its richness. In the midst of all the noise and distractions we may lose our ability to listen to each other and to life, itself. We don't need experts to help us. We need some quiet and time to listen.

Over the years—and it has not been easy—I have learned that quiet listening makes space in me to experience and be formed by God's presence. It opens the possibility for my desires, words, and behavior throughout each day to have their origin in God's presence. Another way of saying this is that quiet listening helps form me as a person of prayer whose life bears manifestations of the mystery of God.

Faithful discernment

You and I ask questions about life, consciously or unconsciously. "Where have I come from?", "Who am I?", "What should my life be like?", and "Where is my life headed?" These recurring questions point toward our need to discern personal meaning and purpose for our lives as long as we live. What are we looking for?

I have a young friend who is at a transition in his life. Recently he spent four days alone in the woods without food on a vision quest. He was sent off by four friends after a ceremony around a camp fire. He experienced doubts and uncertainty that led him to depend on God's Spirit to guide him. He returned to the camp fire without answers, but with resolve to seek opportunities and employment that were congruent with his personal values and his faith in God. His silent solitude and quiet listening, as hard as it was, helped him let go of control of his future and discern what is most important in his life and live according to those values.

My friend's vision quest was similar to Jesus' opportunity for faithful discernment following his baptism.

> *"Now when all the people were baptized, and when Jesus had also been baptized and was praying, the heaven was opened, and the Holy Spirit descended upon him in bodily form like a dove. And a voice came from heaven, 'You are my Son, the Beloved; with you I am well pleased.'"* (Luke 3:21-22) *"Then Jesus was led up by the Spirit into the wilderness to be tempted by the devil. He fasted forty days and forty nights, and afterwards he was famished.* (Matthew 4:1)

Jesus "was praying" at his baptism when the boundary between heaven and earth became transparent. He heard a voice declare that he was God's son and the presence of a dove testified to the intimacy of that relationship. Now he was being led to the desert to be tested and discern what that meant and how this intimate filial relationship with God could be tangible in his life. In the Hebrew scriptures "temptation" means a trial or opportunity to prove one's self, rather than a seduction to wrong doing.

Jesus' prayer in the water of the Jordan led to a time apart in the dry and infertile wilderness. It began with a long period of fasting. In Jesus' culture fasting was an act of self-humiliation called *"taanit"*. (*"When I humbled my soul with fasting..."* Psalm 69:10) It was a form of prayerfully approaching God for God's assistance. This is a clear indication that Jesus realized he needed God's help. His prayer of fasting in the desert seems to have been a direct consequence of his prayer during his baptism. Jesus needed help to discern what *"You are my son"* meant and how that relationship would influence and empower his life and ministry. This would be one of many opportunities in his life of prayer for faithful discernment. The gospel of Luke describes the consequence of Jesus' discernment in the desert: *"Then Jesus, filled with the power of the Spirit, returned to Galilee, and a report about him spread through all the country. He began to teach in their synagogues and was praised by everyone."* (Luke 4:14–15)

Jesus' prayerful experience of his Abba's presence in the desert enabled him to link what he desired for his life and the lives of people around him with discernment of what God desires for human life. His discernment was "faithful" because he trusted his experience of God and was willing to follow where it led. His experiences in prayer became the womb of his words and actions in daily life. *"Do you not believe that I am in the Father and the Father is in me? The words that I say to you I do not speak on my own; but the Father who dwells in me does his works."* (John 14:10)

This kind of discernment involves risk and letting go of control of the outcome of our quiet listening. It is not "blind trust." *It is trust based on our experiences of God day after day, even when nothing seems to be "happening."* It will not come "out of the blue" and requires genuine desire and persistence. The richness of faithful discernment enables a person to see into what is taking place in society and his or her life and find courage to speak and act according to what God desires. Prayer and active involvement in societal issues are colleagues. Trusting God's presence in prayer enables us to trust that God's wisdom and power is present in every situation of our lives.

> *"The disciples gathered around Jesus, and told him all that they had done and taught. He said to them, 'Come away to a deserted place all by yourselves and rest a while.'"* (Mark 6:30–31)

Faithful discernment also requires patient waiting. This is currently counter-cultural. We live in a society of constant information and the desire for hurried, if not instant, results. But information is not knowledge or understanding and results are not always fruitful. Patient waiting makes space for us to listen to God and for the Spirit of God to mentor our thoughts and actions with God's desires for us and the world. Patient waiting opens the door leading to a different experience of time. Chronological time relates to the mind and body's need to find solutions and facilitates "progress," usually with some kind of deadline. Patient waiting helps us accept our limitations and weaknesses, provides persistence in our life of prayer, and develops reliance on God. Amma Syncletica, a fourth-century Christian ascetic in Egypt said, "Eyes see only light. Ears hear only sound, but a listening heart perceives meaning."

"Who am I?", "What should my life be like?", and "Where is my life headed?" Responses to these questions are revealed in the contexts of ordinary, daily life as well as our times of quiet listening. When a person discerns God's presence in the intimacy of prayer, then God's presence can be recognized everywhere. Its hallmark is life-giving power. It is real whenever and wherever it is experienced. Experience of what is real—what is true—in God's presence will unmask what is not real. In our quiet listening Jesus calls us to discern what is real and entrust our lives to the One who is real. This is what Jesus meant when he said: *"You shall know the truth and the truth will make you free."*

We have seen that following Jesus involves trust. Once that commitment is made we learn that Jesus places *his trust in us* to manifest God's life in our daily living. Quiet listening and faithful discernment in daily life lead toward compassionate action in the world around us.

Commitment to the scriptures and life of Jesus' Jewish religious community

In the previous chapter I discussed ways that each us can make a commitment to know and reflect on the Old and New Testaments and participate in the worship and community life of a Christian faith community. Here are some resources for Bible study and simple methods for meditation on the Bible, especially the New Testament and the life of Jesus in the four gospels.

Study of and meditation on the Bible

Study of biblical content is important, but its purpose is not simply information. It is essential, also, to listen to biblical passages without personal agenda and a desired outcome. In this way we can be open to a dialogue with God's Spirit. As we discovered in quiet listening, if we learn to recognize God's voice and presence in the Bible and other sacred scripture we will learn to recognize God's presence and guidance in our daily activities, challenges and relationships. Listening to God in holy scripture—being present in mind, body and spirit—is prayer.

I have listed several books in the Select Bibliography that provide excellent and readable introductions to the Old and New Testaments. They will provide really fine overviews of biblical history and content. If you are interested in this kind of substantive study I suggest you begin with *Jesus: An Historical Approximation* by Jose Antonio Pagola. This book is one of the finest introductions to the life of Jesus in the context of his first-century Jewish culture. After reading Pagola's book I suggest you turn to my book, *Lord, Teach Us To Pray: One Hundred Daily Reflections on Jesus' Life of Prayer.* These daily reflections, based on years of research, will immerse you in Jesus' spiritual formation as a first-century Jew and the myriad ways his prayer became the energy for compassionate engagement in the lives of people around him.

When you have completed the two books mentioned above, I suggest you begin studying the Old Testament. I recommend *Reading The Old Testament: An Introduction (Second Edition)* by Laurence Boadt. This is the most complete and readable introduction to Old Testament content I have ever seen. It will take time to work through it, but I encourage this extra effort. A much shorter introduction is Mark Link's *These Stones Will Shout: A New Voice for the Old Testament.* Sadly, new copies are rarely available, but used copies may be found online. If you have little background in Old Testament study, this is the book to begin your journey.

Reading about the lives and wisdom of faith-filled Christians

We can direct our attention and thought to learning how Jesus was present in the example, prayer and writing of faith-filled women and men whose lives were filled with Jesus' presence. An excellent introduction is *Journey to the Heart: Christian Contemplation*

Through the Centuries. (Edited by Kim Nataraja. New York: Orbis Books, 2011.)It gives short biographies and summaries of the writing of thirty-two women and men, ancient and modern.

Meditation and reflection on passages from the Bible

Meditation and reflection on the Bible, especially the four gospels and the psalms, are essential for persons who want to follow Jesus today. Daily or weekly reading and reflection on portions of the Bible help us remain rooted and grounded in Jesus' life and heritage. When we cannot make sense of what is going on around us in society, daily or weekly personal meditation on portions of the Bible can ground us in the roots of our tradition. If we become grounded in meditation and reflection on scripture and are willing to *listen to the biblical texts* (rather than impose our agenda for study or our search for meaning) we will hear different voices than our own. Both in the liturgy and in personal meditation the Bible will challenge, inspire, and affirm. We will hear its unique spirit-filled wisdom rather than our own voices. We will see ourselves and the world in a light different from the complexities and chaos that surrounds our daily lives. This timeless vision and wisdom will empower us to hear the wisdom of the Holy Spirit and speak the Spirit's voice. We will see ourselves, each other, and the world in a way that is not limited to our personal knowledge and consciousness. We will be empowered to discern and take action in ways we cannot do on our own.

Here is a method for reflecting on portions of the Bible that has been used in the Christian tradition for fifteen-hundred years:

A Simple Form of Lectio Divina
(listening to the Bible in a contemplative way)

- *Lectio Divina* means "divine or sacred reading" and is an ancient form of contemplative prayer found in many religious traditions. In the Christian tradition it has been an essential part of monastic prayer and is now common for Christians in all walks of life. It is a method for using the Bible as a path to contemplation through listening and responding to God's voice in scripture. *Its purpose is listening, rather than abstract analysis or study.* Lectio Divina is an opportunity for you to experience, to be with, and to remain in God; this is a threshold to contemplation and a place where the Holy Spirit leads you beyond saying prayers to become a person of prayer. You will become like the One you experience in prayer.

- Find a relatively quiet place and sit with your back straight, but not rigid.
- Find a brief, perhaps familiar, passage from sacred scripture in your tradition and read it slowly three times with a period of silence after each reading.
- After the first reading, listen for a word or phrase that may attract you in a special way.
- After the second reading, let the passage speak to you personally and respond to what you may hear God saying to you in the passage.
- After the final reading, simply sit in silence for five or ten minutes, without further reflection on the passage, and rest in God's presence and wisdom.
- When your silent period is ended express simple thanks to God.

For learning more about Lectio Divina and suggestions for its use see:

- Thelma Hall. *Too Deep For Words: Rediscovering Lectio Divina (With 500 Scripture Texts for Prayer)*. New York: Paulist Press, 1988 ISBN 0-8091-2959-0
- Norvene Vest. *No Moment Too Small: Rhythms of Silence, Prayer, and Holy Reading*. Kalamazoo: Cistercian Publications, 1994. See Chapter Two. ISBN 1-56101-092-8

A Form of Praying with Scripture called Meletè
(adapted by David Keller from a practice of the desert Mothers and Fathers)

I recommended Meletè as a complement to daily Bible reading or study. Carrying a memorized or written verse to repeat throughout the day will help keep us centered in the midst of what each day brings.

1. After reading or studying portions of the Bible, take some time to sit quietly and come into an awareness of God's presence. Leave your activity of the mind and enter a time of silence and solitude.

2. Choose a short passage (from those you have been studying or reading). Read the passage slowly, aloud if you are alone. Read it three times and then sit quietly, in silence, for five minutes. Avoid the desire to analyze the passage.

3. Take a word or phrase which stands out from the passage and let it enter your heart and mind. Repeat it several times.

4. End your time of solitude with a prayer.

5. Live with the word or phrase for the rest of the day, in the midst of all you do. Memorize the word or phrase or write it down.

6. Just before bedtime recall the word or phrase. If there is time, write some thoughts in your journal. If not, simply recall the word or phrase. In either case, once you have recalled the word or phrase, give it up and let it go. End with a short thanksgiving.

Contemplative Prayer

There are so many voices and fearful situations clamoring for our attention and responses that we have difficulty knowing how and to whom to respond. Who is worthy of our loyalty and efforts? We can become torn and scattered and often feel powerless. What can one person do? Who is in charge? Our vision can become blurred and our energies dissipated. Who and what actions can we trust with such competition for our hearts and minds? Personal prayer is the venue for listening to Jesus who said, *"Make my word your home."* Remaining in God's daily presence is the only way to restore vision and renew energy. Our personal prayer keeps us rooted in

God in the midst of the clamor and chaos of society. And it is the only way to continue to see the natural goodness and sacredness in other people. We will lose hope without this positive vision.

Contemplative prayer, in its variety of forms, has always been and continues to be an essential part of following Jesus and Christian living. Many persons who desire a discipline of contemplative prayer are unaware of its presence in the Christian tradition and look for it in other religious traditions. Here are two simple forms of Christian contemplative prayer.

- **Simple Sitting:** Find a relatively quiet place, if you can. Otherwise use the space available. Sit comfortably with your back straight, but not rigid. With your eyes closed or partially open, begin breathing slowly in and out. Be conscious of your pattern of deep breathing. Let your body and your mind become as relaxed as possible. As your mind becomes relaxed you will experience many thoughts. Let them come and go. Try, as best you can, to let your mind and inner being become empty. Let your whole being be an open vessel for God's presence and voice. Avoid expectations or hoped-for outcomes. Simply be present to God. Some persons repeat a word or short phrase in their mind to help let go of distracting thoughts and bring themselves back to silence of mind. You can choose a word that has special meaning to you. Some persons repeat a name for God such as "Holy One" or a short request such as "Come Holy Spirit". When you have sat in silence for about twenty minutes, open your eyes, wait for a minute or two, give thanks to God and then resume activity.

- **Contemplative Walking:** (This description of contemplative walking is influenced by the teaching of Thich Nhat Hanh, a Zen master in the Vietnamese tradition. For more detail see: *Walking Meditation*. Nguyen Anh-Huong & Thich Nhat Hanh. Boulder: Sounds True, 2006)

  Find a place where you can have relative quiet and space for walking. Or simply use the space at hand. Stand motionless, begin a deep rhythm of breathing and let yourself become relaxed in body, mind and spirit. When you have become centered begin walking. Take small steps with your feet about shoulder's-length apart. Step slowly with a rhythm that allows your feet to alternate touching the ground without stopping between steps. (Remember, there is no right or wrong way.) Continue your deep breathing as you walk.

Remember that each step is the only step and that each moment is the only moment to be in the presence of God. Be aware of each foot's gentle contact with the earth, carpet or floor. Relax your mind and become aware of objects that appear as you walk. Do not try to appreciate or analyze them. Let them be what they are as you encounter them.

Relax your jaw muscles by assuming a half smile. Continue walking without intention, purpose or destination. When distractions or thoughts appear try counting the number of steps you take as you inhale and exhale. This may help restore you to a relaxed attentiveness.

When you wish to end the walking, stop and continue your deep breathing for a minute or two. Offer thanks to God and resume your other activities. Contemplative walking can be very short, but it is best to allow 15-20 minutes. Once in a while try this form of contemplative prayer for an hour outdoors.

Do Not Worry About Results

The purpose of contemplative prayer is to place yourself in the presence of God without agenda or expectations. Do not worry if thoughts come, especially if you are worried, pressured by work to complete, or anxious about a friend or loved-one. Just rest in the quiet of God's love for you. That is enough, even though it may feel that nothing is happening. Entrust yourself to God.

Compassionate engagement with the life of the world

Jesus' life was his message. He moves from quiet listening and discernment in the desert to demonstrate the rushing-in of God's reign through his active and compassionate engagement in people's lives. This was his only purpose and passion.

Jesus made it clear that following him would not be easy and could be costly. *"Then Jesus said to them all, 'If any want to become my followers, let them deny themselves and take up their cross daily and follow me."* (Luke 9:23)

In first-century Israel, persons who followed Jesus took the risk of being associated with a Jewish leader who was extremely popular. Roman authorities could see Jesus' activities as a threat to Roman authority. The punishment for rebellion against Rome was death by crucifixion. What does it mean to "take up a cross daily" in the twenty-first century?

Each modern follower of Jesus will discern "what does following Jesus mean for me?" Here are some questions that I ponder month-to-month that may help with your discernment:

- What are the most urgent needs and challenges that confront my local, the national and international societies at this time in the twenty-first century?
- How will following Jesus Christ enable me to discern a personal response to these needs and challenges?
- What will guide and support me? What may hinder me?

How can anyone possibly do this?

The answer is simple, but the way is not easy. Participating in the life and ministry of Jesus relies on *intimacy with God*. The exhortation of the desert father Abba Paul the Simple says it all: "Keep close to Jesus." Our quiet listening, faithful discernment and active participation in the life of a faith community will form and empower our compassionate engagement in the life of the world. What will help us participate in the life and ministry of Jesus?

Ecology of soul

The Greek word *askeo* means "to take care of something." An *ascetic* person is one who cares for something. *Ascesis* is a pattern or discipline of caring for something we value deeply. Throughout the Christian tradition the "ascetic life" (in a variety of forms) has been valued as a discipline that guides our life with God and reveals God's desires for us and the world. Asceticism is not only for monks; it can be an essential part of the life of every follower of Jesus. It is the way we care for our whole being, that wonderful gift of God. It is caring for and being a steward of: thoughts, words, body, mind and spirit, actions, neighbor, and the earth.

As we have seen, it is possible to live on the surface of life in such a way that we lose touch with the deep-structure of life. In our fast-paced society it is possible to take the care of our soul for granted or, even worse, assume it is unimportant.

A *rule of life* will help us be good stewards of our life with God. What is a rule of life and why is it important? A rule of life is like the Torah that Jesus followed as a devout first-century Jew. It is a teacher helping us walk a path in our life with God. It is freely chosen, not coerced. It is a constant reminder of what is most fundamental in life and helps us be single-minded in our desire to love God and our neighbor. A rule of life provides a combination of prayer, study, meditation, and work. It is a discipline that helps us care for our soul (body, mind, and spirit) and incarnate God's presence in our daily lives. Without a rule of life it is possible that our life with God will get lost or fade in the fast pace, noise, and multiple demands of modern society. It is a stable guide for living that will center our life and prevent intentional or unintentional scattering of our life with God. If you do not have a rule of life begin with a daily or weekly pattern of two or three practices that you consider basic in caring for your soul. Remember that these practices are not ends in themselves. The purpose is remaining in the company of God, not perfection!

Where will following Jesus lead us?

Thomas Merton declares what is most fundamental for a follower of Jesus. *"What we are asked to do at present is not so much to speak of Christ as to let Him live in us so that people may find Him by feeling how He lives in us."*[42]

No one knows where following Jesus will lead. An incident in the first chapter of John's gospel describes an encounter of two disciples of John the Baptist with Jesus. John declares, "Behold the Lamb of God!" and the two men begin to follow Jesus. He turns to them and asks, "What are you looking for?" The men respond, "Rabbi, where are you staying?" Jesus invites them to "Come and see." (John 1:35-39)

A timeless invitation

"Come and See" will evoke a unique response from each person. If we choose to follow Jesus, each step becomes an opportunity for our life to bear the imprint of the presence of God. How will you respond?

Acknowledgements

The seeds for *Reconsidering Jesus of Nazareth* have been germinating for over forty years. I have encountered hundreds of people whose stories of rejection and harmful experiences have left them with doubts about, frustration with, or rejection of the Christian path without getting to know Jesus as a devout first-century Jew. I mention only a few names here because I want to emphasize that this book is written in response to real-life situations. I'm grateful for the honesty and courage of Joe, Robert, Jean, Margaret, Lauren, David, Charlie, Pamela, Alvin, and Aaron.

I could never have written this book earlier in my life and am grateful for mentors who have guided and formed me in so many ways. In high school Robert Clayton and Harold Nichols taught me about the Christian path by the way they lived. I wanted to be like them. In seminary W. Norman Pittenger and Lawrence Rose helped me understand that sharing the significance of Jesus in a complex society requires more than imparting knowledge and must be rooted in a life of prayer. Later in life Jean Dementi showed me that preaching about Jesus becomes effective when it emerges from a pattern of inclusive and pastoral service to other persons. Thomas Hand, S.J. taught me the richness of Christian contemplative experience and ways to listen to the inner voice of the gospels that make Jesus' life real today. Donald Allchin showed me that Jesus calls every human being to make God's life tangible. Larry Todd Wilson helped me identify these people and articulate what means most to me as a priest and teacher and discern ways to share what has been given to me.

I could never have completed this book without the professional manuscript development skills of Maggie Powell, a gifted editor and graphic designer. No author could ask for more. And as always, my wife Emily Wilmer, patiently waited for me to emerge from my writing sprees and offered substantive advice and encouragement. All these people's voices are in this book.

Select bibliography for further study and reflection

The first four books present the life of Jesus as a devout first-century Jew for persons who do not have a background in biblical study or theology. The fifth book by John Shea is a reflection on the consequences of becoming a disciple of Jesus.

Richard Bauckham. *Jesus: A Very Short Introduction*. Oxford: Oxford University Press, 2011.

David G. R. Keller. *Lord, Teach Us To Pray: One Hundred Daily Reflections on Jesus' Life of Prayer*. Eugene, OR: Cascade Books, 2015.

José A. Pagola. *Jesus: An Historical Approximation*. Miami: Convivium Press, 2009.

Donald Senior. *Jesus: A Gospel Portrait*. Mahwah: Paulist Press, 1992.

John Shea. *Following Jesus*. Maryknoll, New York: Orbis Books, 2010.

Mark Link's *These Stone Will Shout* gives a relatively short, yet well-informed, overview of the Old Testament that will lead to prayerful reflection.

Laurence Boadt's *Reading The Old Testament: An Introduction. Second Edition* is a detailed, yet well-organized, introduction to the Old Testament. Boadt's style is very readable. It is, by far, the best substantive introduction to the Hebrew Scriptures in print.

Mark Link. *These Stone Will Shout: A New Voice for the Old Testament*. Allen, Texas: Tabor Publishing, Second Revised Edition, 1983.

Lawrence Boadt. *Reading The Old Testament: An Introduction. Second Edition,* Revised and Updated by Richard Clifford and Daniel Harrington. New York: Paulist Press, 2012.

Resources

Electronic and World-Wide-Web Resources

Cell phone and email daily meditation sites

- Prayasyougo.org is a website maintained by the Jesuits of Great Britain that provides *daily podcasts*. Prayerful meditations on scripture complete with musical selections from different parts of the world, are provided in a well-structured ten–fifteen minute program (Monday through Friday each week).

- dailyreflections@csbsju.edu is a short and streetwise daily blog by Fr. Don Talafous, OSB. Fr. Don is a Benedictine monk who has lived among young adults at St. John's University all of his adult life. He is wise, often humorous, and very down-to-earth.

- Explorefaith.org offers spiritual guidance for anyone seeking a path to God. Its resources for various forms of prayer and meditation are especially helpful and have appeal across denominational traditions. It offers a really fine weekly email newsletter (free) featuring prayers, reflections and "tools for the journey."

- Gratefulness.org is a website with a rich variety of resources that remind us of the fundamental importance of gratefulness in our lives. It is centered on the teaching of Brother David Steindl-Rast, O.S.B. It offers a free daily e-mail "Word for the Day."

- HenriNouwen.org will give you access to a free daily meditation from the wisdom of Henri Nouwen, one of the most profound and influential Roman Catholic spiritual writers of the twentieth century. His reflections appeal to persons from a variety of backgrounds.

Christian contemplative prayer and meditation web-sites

For information about Christian meditation groups inspired by John Main, OSB and Lawrence Freeman OSB consult the World Community for Christian Meditation at www.wccm.org Other web sites include:

- www.johnmainprayer.com
- www.laycontemplative.org/world_community.htm

Daily reading from the Bible

The Revised Common Lectionary is a resource for finding Sunday and daily readings from the Bible. The web address is:

- https://lectionary.library.vanderbilt.edu//

Daily reading from a variety of religious traditions

The best collection of daily readings from a variety of religious traditions that I have used is *God Makes the Rivers to Flow: Passages for meditation.* Selected by Eknath Easwaren. Petaluma, CA: Nilgiri Press, 1982.

Praying the Hours

(Adapted from David Keller. Come and See: The Transformation of Personal Prayer. *Harrisburg: Morehouse Publishing, 2009)*

Many Christian monastic communities follow a rhythm of prayer and meditation that enables them to remain in the company of God in the midst of other important activities in each day. These are called the *monastic hours* and usually include pausing for prayer and meditation from four to seven times a day. Here are two very simple alternatives for the beginning and end of each day inspired by the monastic hours. You are encouraged to develop your own "Book of Hours" based on your work schedule and life style. The morning and evening "hours" intentionally place you in God's presence at the beginning and ending of each day and remind you that you are loved unconditionally. When you begin each day knowing you are loved you will eventually develop an attitude of gratefulness that will influence every aspect of your daily relationships and tasks. If you end each day in the awareness of God's love you will be able offer that day as a gift, aware of accomplishments and pleasures as well as failures or missed opportunities. Offering yourself to God at the end of the day will help you accept yourself, remind you of the sanctity of your life, and help you rely on God for newness of life. It will also help you rest and rise in the new day!

A Morning Hour: Matins

Soon after waking and rising and in a manner that is comfortable for you, let your body express a sense of gratefulness for the new day and an openness to God's presence. You may want to say this ancient prayer from the Psalms:

> *O Holy One, open my lips*
> *that my mouth may declare your praise.*

Then, using a Bible or collection of sacred texts, read a short passage and then reflect on it for one or two minutes. (Remember that you can use https://lectionary.library.vanderbilt.edu// to find selections if you are unsure what to choose.)

Read the passage again, followed by a short period of silence.

Then, you may decide to articulate your personal concerns or prayers for situations, persons, and the life of the world.

Bring your morning "hour" to a close with this ancient prayer:

> *Bind my head and my heart in you, Holy One,*
> *and may I remain in your company this day.*

Or you may use this prayer adapted from a prayer of Saint Paul:

> *The grace of Jesus Christ, the love of God, and the companionship*
> *of the Holy Spirit be with me in each moment of this day.*

Or this prayer from St. Patrick of Ireland (387–460)

May the strength of God guide me this day,
And may God's power preserve me.
May the wisdom of God instruct me,
And the eye of God watch over me.
May the ear of God hear me,
And the word of God give sweetness to my speech.
May the hand of God defend me,
And may I follow the way of God.

You may want to carry the scripture passage from Matins with you throughout the day and let it speak to you consciously or unconsciously.

An Evening Hour: Vespers

After supper or before getting ready for bed spend a short period of time in silence. Then begin Vespers with this prayer adapted from the Psalms:

O God come to my assistance,
O Holy One make haste to help me.

Then, using a Bible or collection of sacred texts, read a short passage and then reflect on it for one or two minutes. Read the passage again and pause briefly.

Then, you may decide to articulate your personal concerns or prayers for situations, persons, and the life of the world.

Bring your evening "hour" to a close with this ancient prayer:

Into your hands, O God, I entrust my spirit.

You will find, in time, that being aware of God's presence and commending your life to God first thing in the morning and again in the evening will become a strong foundation for each day, regardless of what the day brings into your life. The power of personal prayer is that it will keep you rooted and grounded in God rather than yourself.

Your inner self,
the unfading beauty
of a gentle and quiet spirit,
is of great worth in God's sight.

The New Testament First Letter of Saint Peter
Chapter 3, verse 4

Sources used by the author

American Bible Society. *Revised Standard Version Synopsis of the Four Gospels*. New York: American Bible Society, 2010.

Kenneth E. Bailey. *Jesus Through Middle Eastern Eyes: Cultural Studies in the Gospels*. Downers Grove: IVP Academic, 2008.

Samuel E. Balentine. *Prayer in the Hebrew Bible: The Drama of Divine-Human Dialog*. Minneapolis: Fortress Press, 1993.

Bruno Barnhart. *The Good Wine: Reading John from the Center*. Mahwah, N.J.: Paulist Press, 1993.

David Biven. *New Light on the Difficult Words of Jesus: Insights from His Jewish Context*. Holland, MI: En-Gedi Resource Center, 2007.

Matthew Black. *An Aramaic Approach to the Gospels and Acts*. Hendrickson Publishers, 1998.

Lawrence Boadt. *Reading The Old Testament: An Introduction. Second Edition*, Revised and Updated by Richard Clifford and Daniel Harrington. New York: Paulist Press, 2012.

Marcus Borg. *Jesus A New Vision: Spirit, Culture, and the Life of Discipleship*. San Francisco: Harper and Row, 1987.

Günther Bornkamm. *Jesus of Nazareth*. Minneapolis: Fortress Press, 1995.

Bruce Chilton. *Jesus' Prayer and Jesus' Eucharist: His Personal Practice of Spirituality*. Valley Forge, PA: Trinity Press International, 1997.

Bernard J. Cooke, *God's Beloved, Jesus' Experience of the Transcendent*. Philadelphia: Trinity Press International, 1992.

John Dominic Crossan and Jonathan L. Reed. *Excavating Jesus: Beneath the Stones, Behind the Texts*. San Francisco: HarperSanFrancisco, 2001.

Adriana Destro and Mauro Pesce. *Encounters With Jesus: The Man in His Place and Time*. Minneapolis: Fortress Press, 2012.

Samuel H. Dresner, ed. *I Asked For Wonder: A Spiritual Anthology Abraham Joshua Heschel*. New York: Crossroad, 1986.

James D. G. Dunn. *Jesus and the Spirit*. Grand Rapids: Eerdmans Publishing Company, 1975.

_____. *Jesus Remembered.* Grand Rapids: Eerdmans Publishing Company, 2003.

_____. *A New Perspective on Jesus: What the Quest for the Historical Jesus Missed.* Grand Rapids: Baker Academic, 2005.

_____. *Jesus, Paul, and the Gospels.* Grand Rapids: Eerdmans Publishing Company, 2011.

David Flusser. *The Sage from Galilee: Rediscovering Jesus' Genius.* Grand Rapids: Eerdmans Publishing Company, Fourth English Edition 2007.

Thelma Hall. *Too Deep For Words: Rediscovering Lectio Divina.* New York: Paulist Press, 1988.

Herschel Shanks, ed. *Partings: How Judaism and Christianity Became Two.* Washington, D.C.: Biblical Archaeology Society, 2014.

Kenneth C. Hanson and Douglas E. Oakman. *Palestine in the Time of Jesus: Social Structures and Social Conflicts. Second Edition.* Minneapolis: Fortress Press, 2008.

Daniel Harrington, S.J. *Jesus and Prayer: What the New Testament Teaches Us.* Word Among Us Press, 2009.

Patrick J. Hartin. *Exploring the Spirituality of the Gospels.* Collegeville: Liturgical Press, 2010.

Joseph Heinemann with Jacob J. Petuchowski. *Literature of the Synagogue.* Piscataway, NJ: Gorgias, 2006.

Nguyen Anh-Huong & Thich Nhat Hanh. *Walking Meditation.* Boulder: Sounds True, 2006.

Joachim Jeremias. *Prayers of Jesus.* Eugene: Wipf and Stock Publishers, 1978, 2006 (reprint).

_____. *Jerusalem in the Time of Jesus.* Philadelphia: Fortress Press, 1975 edition.

Craig S. Keener. *The Historical Jesus of the Gospels.* Grand Rapids: Eerdmans Publishing Company, 2009.

David G. R. Keller. *Oasis of Wisdom: The Worlds of the Desert Mothers and Fathers.* Collegeville: Liturgical Press, 2005.

_____. *Come and See: The Transformation of Personal Prayer.* Harrisburg: Morehouse Publishing, 2009

_____. *Desert Banquet: A Year of Wisdom from the Desert Mothers and Fathers.* Collegeville: Liturgical Press, 2011.

_____ . *Boundless Grandeur: The Christian Vision of A. M. Donald Allchin.* Eugene, OR: Pickwick Publications, 2015.

_____. *Lord, Teach Us To Pray: One Hundred Daily Reflections on Jesus' Life of Prayer.* Eugene, OR: Cascade Books, 2015.

John Koenig. *Rediscovering New Testament Prayer: Boldness and Blessing in the Name of Jesus.* San Francisco: HarperSanFrancisco, 1992.

Bernard J. Lee, S.M. *The Galilean Jewishness of Jesus: Retrieving the Jewish Origins of Christianity.* Mahwah: Paulist Press, 1988.

Mark Link. *These Stones Will Shout: A New Voice for the Old Testament.* Allen, Texas: Tabor Publishing, Second Revised Edition, 1983.

Eli Lizorkin-Eyzenberg. *The Jewish Gospel of John.* Tel Mond, Israel. Israel Study Center, 2015.

Gerhard Lohfink. *Jesus of Nazareth: What He Wanted, Who He Was.* Collegeville: Liturgical Press, 2012.

Bruce J. Malina. *The New Testament World: Insights from Cultural Anthropology,* third edition. Louisville: Westminster John Knox Press, 2001.

Bruce J. Malina and Richard L. Rohrbaugh. *Social-Science Commentary on the Synoptic Gospels.* Minneapolis: Augsburg Fortress Press, 2003.

George A. Maloney, SJ, trans. *Intoxicated With God: The Fifty Spiritual Homilies of Macarius.* Denville: Dimension Books, 1978.

Frederick Murphy. *Early Judaism: The Exile to the Time of Christ.* Peabody, Mass.: Hendrickson Publishing, 2002, 2006.

Jerome Murphy-O'Connor, O.P. *Becoming Human Together: The Pastoral Anthropology of St. Paul.* Atlanta: Society of Biblical Literature, third edition , 2009.

Kim Nataraja, ed., *Journey to the Heart: Christian Contemplation Through the Centuries.* New York: Orbis Books, 2011.

José A. Pagola. *Jesus: An Historical Approximation.* Miami: Convivium Press, 2009.

Johs. Pedersen. *Israel: Its Life And Culture.* Vol. III-IV. London: Oxford University Press, 1940.

Norman Perrin. *Jesus and the Language of the Kingdom: Symbol and Metaphor in New Testament Interpretation.* Philadelphia: Fortress Press, 1976.

John J. Pilch. *The Cultural World of Jesus, Sunday by Sunday, Cycle A.* Collegeville: Liturgical Press, 1995.

_____. *The Cultural World of Jesus, Sunday by Sunday, Cycle B.* Collegeville: Liturgical Press, 1996.

_____. *The Cultural World of Jesus, Sunday by Sunday, Cycle C.* Collegeville: Liturgical Press, 1996.

Pheme Perkins. *Jesus As Teacher.* Cambridge: Cambridge University Press, 1990.

Karl Rahner. *Encounters With Silence.* Westminster, MD.: Christian Classics, 1984.

John Riches. *The World of Jesus.* Cambridge: Cambridge University Press, 1990.

James M. Robinson. *The Sayings of Jesus: The Sayings Gospel Q in English.* Minneapolis: Fortress Press, 2002.

John J. Rousseau and Rami Arav. *Jesus and His World: An Archaeological and Cultural Dictionary.* Minneapolis: Fortress Press, 1995.

Donald Senior. *Jesus: A Gospel Portrait.* Mahwah: Paulist Press, 1992.

Jens Schröter. *Jesus of Nazareth: Jew From Galilee, Savior Of The World.* Waco: Baylor University Press, 2014.

H. Stephen Shoemaker. *Finding Jesus in His Prayers.* Nashville: Abingdon Press, 2004.

Ethelbert Stauffer. *Jesus and His Story.* London: SCM Press LTD, 1960.

Robert H. Stein. *The Method and Message of Jesus' Teachings.* Louisville: Westminster John Knox Press, 1994.

Rabbir Eliezer Toledano, ed. *The Orot Sephardic Weekday Siddur.* Lakewood, NJ: Orot Inc., 1995.

Geza Vermes. *The Religion of Jesus the Jew.* Minneapolis: Augsburg Fortress, 1993.

_____. *The Authentic Gospel of Jesus.* New York: Penguin Books, 2004.

Norvene Vest. *No Moment Too Small: Rhythms of Silence, Prayer, and Holy Reading.* Kalamazoo: Cistercian Publications, 1994.

Ben Witherington III. *The Jesus Quest: The Third Search for The Jew of Nazareth.* Downers Grove: InterVarsity Press, 1997.

N.T. Wright. *Jesus and the Victory of God.* Minneapolis: Augsburg Press, 1996.

_____. *The Challenge of Jesus: Rediscovering Who Jesus Was and Is.* Downers Grove: InterVarsity Press, 1999.

Brad H. Young. *Meet The Rabbis: Rabbinic Thought and the Teachings of Jesus.* Grand Rapids, MI: Baker Academic, 2007.

Esther de Wall. *A Seven Day Journey With Thomas Merton.* Ann Arbor: Servant Publications, 1992.

Endnotes

1. Genesis 1:31

2. Genesis 1:27

3. The First Letter of John 1:8 in the New Testament.

4. Ezekiel 18:23

5. Isaiah 31:3

6. John 8:1-11

7. *Intoxicated With God: The Fifty Spiritual Homilies of Macarius.* Translated by George A. Maloney, SJ. Denville: Dimension Books, 1978. Homily 11, page 82.

8. *I Asked For Wonder: A Spiritual Anthology Abraham Joshua Heschel.* Edited by Samuel H. Dresner. New York: Crossroad, 1986. pages 20 and 22.

9. For a detailed study of this topic by Jewish and Christian scholars see: *Partings: How Judaism and Christianity Became Two.* Herschel Shanks, editor. Washington, D.C. : Biblical Archaeology Society, 2014.

10. I am indebted to Raimon Panikkar for my understanding of Christness, a term I learned from him. It is his firm belief that Christian faith communities, usually called denominations or churches, are not ends in themselves. They exist to form persons into manifestations of Jesus' presence in the world today.

11. Quoted in David G. R. Keller. *Oasis of Wisdom: The Worlds of the Desert Mothers and Fathers.* Collegeville: Liturgical Press, 2005, 54.

12. I am indebted to my mentor, A. M. Donald Allchin, for these insights about God's presence in our lives. I describe Donald's emphasis on participation in God's life in my commentary on his book, *Participation in God.* See: David G. R. Keller, "Donald Allchin's Understanding of the Mystery of the Life of God in Humankind," in *Boundless Grandeur: The Christian Vision of A. M. Donald Allchin.* David Keller, ed., Pickwick Publications: Eugene, OR, 2015, 97-110.

13. "Thus he has given us, through these things, his precious and very great promises, so that through them you may escape from the corruption in the world because of lust, and may become participants of the divine nature." (2 Peter 1:4)

14. I have chosen to concentrate on the way the four canonical gospels record Jesus' deep consciousness of God because they give more complete narratives of Jesus daily life and encounters with people as well as accounts of the last week of his life, his death, resurrection and risen life among his followers.

15. A. M. Donald Allchin, *Participation in God*, 76. Quoted in David G. R. Keller. *Boundless Grandeur: The Christian Vision of A. M. Donald Allchin.* Eugene: Pickwick Publications, 2015, 110.

16. The four New Testament gospels are called gospels because they present Jesus' life and teaching in the context of his daily activities and relationships and include details from the last week of his life, his resurrection, and a variety of appearances to disciples after his resurrection. The gospels include narratives that represent eye-witness responses to incidents in Jesus' life as well as narratives influenced by the disciples' experience of Jesus after his resurrection.

17. David began his life as a shepherd. He became a skilled military commander under Saul, Israel's first king. The prophet Samuel anointed David King after the death of Saul and David was able to unite the various tribes of the Israelites. One of his successful and wise accomplishments was to conquer the city of Jerusalem from the Canaanites and make it both the political and religious center of Israel. At the same time, although his faith in God was firm, David was a flawed human being. He assured that one of his military commanders would be killed in battle so that David could marry his wife. He favored his son, Absalom, to such a degree that Absalom almost succeeded in a revolt against David to gain his throne. Yet David was remembered a king that united Israel and whose son, Solomon, extended the boundaries of Israel and ensured its dominance as a nation. Israelites believe that "The House of David" was ordained by God and would continue without end.

18. This symbolic connection to "The House of David" takes on added importance because at the time of Jesus' birth Israel was occupied by the Roman Empire and there was growing hope that God would intervene to restore Israel's independence.

19. See Isaiah 42:1–9.

20. The gospel narratives describe many visits of angels and discernment through dreams. First-century people took dreams and angelic visits very seriously, whereas we in the twenty-first century tend to discount things that cannot be verified rationally.

21. See Isaiah 42:1–9; Micah 6:6–8 & 7:18–20; Psalm 36:5–9; and Amos 5:24 as a few examples.

22. The exact date is not known, but relating the context of John's activity to historical data in Roman and Jewish history seems to confirm this date. See Ethelbert Stauffer. *Jesus and His Story,* 51–55; 59.

23. David G. R. Keller. *Lord, Teach Us To Pray: One Hundred Daily Reflections on Jesus' Life of Prayer.* Eugene, OR: Cascade Books, 2015, 32

24. Quoted in David Biven. *New Light on the Difficult Words of Jesus: Insights from His Jewish Context*. Holland, MI: En-Gedi Resource Center, 2007, 128.

25. Op cit., 128.

26. I am grateful to Günther Bornkamm, of of the most respected twenti-eth-century New Testament scholars, for this insight. For more details see: Günther Bornkamm. *Jesus of Nazareth*. Minneapolis: Fortress Press, 1995, chapter IV.

27. Excerpted from David G. R. Keller. *Lord, Teach Us To Pray: One Hundred Daily Reflections on Jesus' Life of Prayer*. Eugene, OR: Cascade Books, 2015, 46.

28. Op cit., 46–47.

29. See: David Flusser. *The Sage from Galilee: Rediscovering Jesus' Genius*. Grand Rapids: Eerdmans, 2007, 94.

30. The Passover was and continues to be a major Jewish feast celebrating the escape of the Hebrews from slavery in Egypt during the time of Moses, their wandering in the wilderness of Sinai, and the covenant they made with God at Mt. Sinai. This covenant bonded them with God and the Law given by God at Sinai was a guide for living according to their commit-ment to God.

31. I acknowledge the scholarship of Bruno Barnhart for this interpreta-tion of the foot washing incident. See Bruno Barnhart. *The Good Wine: Reading John from the Center*. Mahwah, N.J.: Paulist Press, 1993, 120–128.

32. I am grateful to Bruno Barnhart for this insight.

33. Sometimes translated "kingdom" or "realm" of God.

34. Johs. Pedersen. *Israel: Its Life And Culture*. Vol. III-IV. London: Oxford University Press, 1940, rev. 1949. Page 323

35. I am grateful for the scholarship of Johs. Pedersen for my understanding of Israelite sacrifice. See Johs. Pedersen. *Israel, Its Life And Culture*, Vols. III-IV. London: Oxford University Press, 1940, 302–326.

36. Jerome Murphy-O'Connor, O.P. *Becoming Human Together: The Pastoral Anthropology of St. Paul*. Atlanta: Society of Biblical Literature, 2009 third edition. P. 188

37. Karl Rahner. *Encounters With Silence*. Westminster, Md.: Christian Classics, 1984, 29.

38. Wisdom of Solomon 9:13

39. 1 Corinthians 2:11

40. *An Interrupted Life: The Diaries and Letters of Etty Hillesum 1941–1943,* introduction by J.G. Gaarlandt, translation by Arnold J. Pomerans. New York: Pantheon Books, 1984.

41. This paragraph is based on portions of Chapter 10 in my book *Come and See: The Transformation of Personal Prayer*

42. Quoted by Esther de Wall in *A Seven Day Journey With Thomas Merton.* Ann Arbor: Servant Publications, 1992, 29.

About David Keller

David Keller is an Episcopal priest who spent the first 20 years of his ministry with Athabaskan Indians and Yupic and Inupiat Eskimos in Alaska. He worked alongside Alaskan Native leaders in community development projects and developing training for local people for lay and ordained ministries. Later, David was the Director of the Bishop's School for Ministry Development for the Episcopal Church in Arizona and then Director of the Episcopal House of Prayer at St. John's Abbey in Collegeville, MN. He has led retreats throughout the USA and UK and taught in the Center for Christian Spirituality at the General Theological Seminary in New York City. David is the author of *Come and See: The Transformation of Personal Prayer* and *Lord, Teach Us To Pray: One Hundred Daily Reflections on Jesus' Life of Prayer*.

With his wife, Emily Wilmer, he directs Oasis of Wisdom:
A Center for Contemplative Living
www.oasisofwisdom.net